# ENGLISH in Common

## Workbook

Jonathan Bygrave

Series Consultants
María Victoria Saumell and Sarah Louisa Birchley

ALWAYS LEARNING

**PEARSON**

English in Common 1
Workbook

Pearson Education, 10 Bank Street, White Plains, NY 10606

**Staff credits:** The editorial, design, production, and
manufacturing people who make up the *English in Common 1*
team are Margaret Antonini, Allen Ascher, Rhea Banker, Eleanor
Kirby Barnes, Mike Boyle, Tracey Cataldo, Aerin Csigay, Dave
Dickey, Chris Edmonds, Stacey Hunter, Mike Kemper, Loretta
Steeves, Leigh Stolle, Katherine Sullivan, and Charlie Green.

This series is dedicated to Charlie Green. Without Charlie's
knowledge of pedagogy, strong work ethic, sense of humor,
patience, perseverance, and creativity, *English in Common* would
never have existed.

Cover design: Tracey Cataldo
Cover photo: © qushe/shutterstock.com
Text design: Tracey Cataldo
Text composition: TSI Graphics
Text font: MetaPlus

ISBN 13: 978-0-13-262864-8
ISBN 10: 0-13-262864-3

**Library of Congress Cataloging-in-Publication Data**
Bygrave, Jonathan
    English in common. Book 1 / Jonathan Bygrave.
        p. cm.
    ISBN 0-13-247003-9—ISBN 0-13-262725-6—
ISBN 0-13-262727-2—ISBN 0-13-262728-0—
ISBN 0-13-262729-9—ISBN 0-13-262731-0
1. English language—Textbooks for foreign speakers.
2. English language—Grammar.
3. English language—Spoken English.
    PE1128.B865 2011
    428.24--dc23

2011024736

Printed in the United States of America
1 2 3 4 5 6 7 8 9 10—V001—16 15 14 13 12

**Photo Credits:** Page 6 (all) PunchStock; p. 9 (1) Press Association
Images, (2) Shutterstock.com, (3) Frazer Harrison/Getty Images,
(4) Camera Press Ltd., p. 10 Lucas Jackson/Reuters/Corbis;
p. 11 (A) Pearson Education, (B) PunchStock, (C) PunchStock,
(D) PunchStock; p. 13 PunchStock; p. 14 (1) PunchStock, (2) Mikael
Karlsson/Alamy, (3) Blend Images/Alamy, (4) PunchStock,
(5) Shutterstock.com, (6) Dan Tardif/Corbis, (7) Christian Hoehn/
Getty Images, (8) Chris Ryan/Getty Images, (9) Shutterstock.com,
(top right) Shutterstock.com, (bottom right) PunchStock; p. 15
(1) PunchStock, (2) Butch Martin/Getty Images, (3) PunchStock,
(4) PunchStock, (5) Jim Powell/Alamy, (6) Michael Prince/Corbis,
(7) PunchStock; p. 16 (A) Car Photo Library, (B) Courtesy of Canon,
(C) Douglas Pilsipher/Alamy, (D) PunchStock, (E) Courtesy of
Phillips; p. 17 PunchStock; p. 21 (left) Nik Wheeler/Corbis,
(A) Shutterstock.com, (B) Catherine Desjeux/Corbis, (C) Courtesy
of New York Museum of Contemporary Art; p. 26 (4, 5, 6, 7)
Shutterstock.com; p. 27 Shutterstock.com; p. 28 (top left & right)
PunchStock, (middle left) PunchStock, (middle right) Camera
Press Ltd., (bottom left & right) PunchStock; p. 31 Shutterstock.com;
p. 32 (1) PunchStock, (4) PunchStock, (7) PunchStock,
(10) Imageshop/Alamy; p. 34 Rex Features; p. 37 (left) Leland
Bobbe/Corbis, (right) PunchStock, (middle) PunchStock, (bottom)
Rex Features; p. 39 (left) PunchStock, (right) Shutterstock.com;
p. 40 Jim Graigmyle/Corbis; p. 45 Shutterstock.com; p. 47 (A)
Shutterstock.com, (B) Shutterstock.com, (C) PunchStock;
p. 51 (top left) TIPS Images, (bottom left) Shutterstock.com,
(right) SuperStock; p. 52 Work Book Stock/Getty Images;
p. 53 Shutterstock.com; p. 54 (top) PunchStock, (bottom) Dominic
Dibbs/Anthony Blake Photo Library; p. 55 Iconica/Getty Images;
p. 56 (top right) Hulton Archive/Getty Images, (middle right)
V&A Images; p. 57 Bettmann/Corbis; p. 58 Rex Features;
p. 62 (1) Neil Guegan/Corbis, (2) Reuters, (3) DK Images, (4) Ian
M. Butterfield/Alamy; p. 63 (left) The Bridgeman Art Library Ltd/
Self Portrait, 1887 (oil on canvas), Gogh, Vincent van (1853–90)/
Musée d'Orsay, Paris, France, (right) The Bridgeman Art Library
Ltd/Breton Peasants, 1894 (oil on canvas), Gauguin, Paul
(1848–1903)/Lauros/Giraudon, Musée d'Orsay, Paris, France;
p. 64 Press Association Images; p. 65 (top) PunchStock;
p. 67 iStockphoto.com.

**Illustration Credits:** Beach; F&L Productions; Gary Kaye;
Graham Kennedy; Joanne Kerr (New Division); Lucy Truman (New
Division); Mark Duffin; Roger Penwill.

# Contents

# UNIT 1
# Introductions

## Speaking

**1a** Complete the conversations with words from the box.

> | | | | |
> |---|---|---|---|
> | Welcome | too | name | Hi |
> | Thank | I'm | ~~Nice~~ | |

1. A: Hello. I'm Rick Lane. _Nice_ to meet you.

   B: Nice to meet you, _____ .

2. A: Hi, Mona.

   B: _____ , Andre.

3. A: Good morning.

   B: _____ to Mercer Hotel.

   A: _____ you.

4. A: Hello. I'm Charles Reed. What's your _____ ?

   B: _____ Taku Suzuki.

**b** Match the conversations in Exercise 1a to the pictures.

Conversation _____

Conversation _1_

Conversation _____

Conversation _____

## Vocabulary

**2** Complete the crossword puzzle. Spell the numbers.

| Across → | Down ↓ |
|---|---|
| ~~c 1~~ | ~~a 2~~ |
| e 5 | b 8 |
| g 6 | d 4 |
| h 3 | f 7 |
| i 9 | |

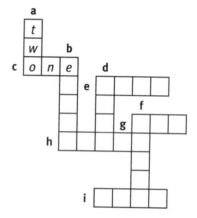

## Communication

**3** Write the room numbers.

1.

   _four three eight_

2. 534

   _____

3. 702

   _____

4. 619

   _____

5. 111

   _____

# Grammar

**4** Look at the information. Complete the conversations.

1.

NAME    David Franks
ROOM    601

A: Hello. Welcome to the
   _Linton Hotel_ .
B: Thank you. _I'm David Franks_ .
A: _You're in room 601_ , Mr. Franks.

2.

Name    Susan Jackson
Room    329

A: Hello. Welcome to the _____.
B: Thank you. _____.
A: _____, Ms. Jackson.

3.

Name    Ricardo Mendoza
Room    540

A: Hello. Welcome to the _____.
B: Thank you. _____.
A: _____, Mr. Mendoza.

**5** Correct the mistakes in the conversations.

1. A: Hello. (I)Silvia Rodriguez.
     I'm
   B: Hello, Ms. Rodriguez.

2. A: Good morning, Mr. Nakamura. You in room 922.
   B: Thank you.

3. A: Hello. Im Jin Chang.
   B: Im Farah Coleman.

4. A: I'm John Wilson.
   B: Hello, Mr. Wilson. Youre in room 102.

# Vocabulary

**6** Use each picture to write a conversation below.

A   <u>7:30</u>
Henry:             Good morning, Ms. Sharapova.
Maria Sharapova:    _Good morning_ , _Henry_ .

B   <u>3:30</u>
Henry:        _____, _____.
Leonardo DiCaprio:   _____, _____.

C   <u>7:30</u>
Henry:        _____, _____.
Gwyneth Paltrow:   _____, _____.

D   <u>11:00</u>
Henry:        _____, _____.
Jamie Foxx:     _____, _____.

**7** Use the phrases in the box to write a conversation.

| | |
|---|---|
| I'm Polly Tiller | Nice to meet you |
| ~~Good morning~~ | I'm Evan Larson |
| Good morning | Nice to meet you, too |

Evan:   _Good morning_ .
Polly: _____.
Evan: _____.
Polly: _____.
Evan: _____.
Polly: _____.

# Vocabulary

**1** Read the chart. Then write the number of the vowel sound below each letter.

|  | Vowel sound | Example |
|---|---|---|
| **1.** | /eɪ/ | <u>eig</u>ht |
| **2.** | /i/ | thr<u>ee</u> |
| **3.** | /ɛ/ | t<u>e</u>n |
| **4.** | /aɪ/ | f<u>i</u>ve |
| **5.** | /oʊ/ | zer<u>o</u> |
| **6.** | /u/ | tw<u>o</u> |
| **7.** | /ɑ/ | <u>a</u>re |

*a*   *b*   *c*   *d*
 1    2    2   ___

*e*   *f*   *g*   *h*
___  ___  ___  ___

*i*   *j*   *k*   *l*
___  ___  ___  ___

*m*   *n*   *o*   *p*
___  ___  ___  ___

*q*   *r*   *s*   *t*
___  ___  ___  ___

*u*   *v*   *w*   *x*
___  ___  ___  ___

*y*   *z*
___  ___

**2a** Correct the spelling and underline the stress.

1. Japon _*Japan*_
2. Chna _____
3. Mexica _____
4. Germane _____
5. Australya _____
6. The KU _____
7. Argantina _____
8. Brazil _____

**b** Complete the puzzle to find the country name. Use Exercise 2a to help you.

1.    2.

3.    4.

5.    6.

7.

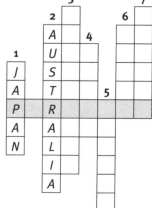

# Grammar

**3** Write sentences with *He's*, *She's*, or *It's*.

1. Sergio
   _*He's Sergio*_.

2. Amy
   _____.

3. Francesca
   _____.

4. New York
   _____.

5. London
   _____.

6. Rico
   _____.

**4**  Write two sentences for each picture.

US

1. _He's from Brazil_ .
   _He's in the US_ .

the UK

2. She _____ .
   _____ .

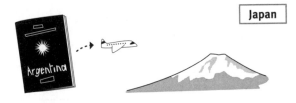

Japan

3. He _____ .
   _____ .

Australia

4. He _____ .
   _____ .

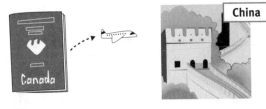

China

5. She _____ .
   _____ .

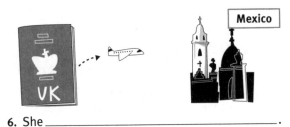

Mexico

6. She _____ .
   _____ .

# Reading

**5**  Read the conversation. Then complete the details about the people.

| | |
|---|---|
| Candy: | Hello. I'm Candy Banks. |
| Paul: | Hello, Candy. I'm Paul Earle. |
| Candy: | Nice to meet you, Paul. |
| Paul: | Nice to meet you, too. Look, she's Adriana. |
| Candy: | Adriana? |
| Paul: | Yes. Adriana Rios. She's from Fort Lauderdale. |
| Candy: | In the UK? |
| Paul: | No. Fort Lauderdale is in Florida, in the US. |
| Candy: | Oh. |
| Receptionist: | Mr. Earle? |
| Paul: | Yes. |
| Receptionist: | Good morning, Mr. Earle. Welcome to Fortune Hotel. |
| Paul: | Thank you. |
| Receptionist: | You're in room eight nine one. |
| Paul: | OK. Thanks. |
| Receptionist: | And Ms. Banks? |
| Candy: | Yes. |
| Receptionist: | Welcome to Fortune Hotel, Ms. Banks. You're in room six one four. |
| Candy: | Thank you. |

1.

Name: _____
From: _____

2.

Name: _____
Room: _____

3.

Name: _____
Room: _____

## Vocabulary

**1a** Complete the words and phrases.

1. S_o_rry.
2. P__rd__n?
3. N__, th__nk y____.
4. N__c__ t__ m____t y____.
5. __xc__s__ m__.
6. Y__s, pl____s__.

**b** Match the phrases from Exercise 1a to the pictures.

A

B

C

D _1_

E

F

## Communication

**2** Complete the introductions of:

1. Nicole and Keith

   You: _Nicole, this is Keith_ .

   Nicole: _Nice to meet you, Keith_ .

   Keith: _Nice to meet you too, Nicole_ .

2. Colin and Laura

   You: _____ .

   Colin: _____ .

   Laura: _____ .

3. Harry and Mary

   You: _____ .

   Harry: _____ .

   Mary: _____ .

## Grammar

**3** Put the words in the correct order.

**Theo:** is/Ali/this/Carol,
   _Carol, this is Ali_ .

**Carol:** meet/to/Nice/you

   _____ .

**Ali:** meet/to/too/you,/Nice

   _____ .

**Carol:** from,/Where/Ali/are/you

   _____ ?

**Ali:** from/UK/the/I'm

   _____ .

**Carol:** you/are/from/Where/the UK/in

   _____ ?

**Ali:** from/London/I'm

   _____ .

**4** Complete the conversations.

1. **A:** Where _____are_____ you ____from____ in the US?

   **B:** I'm from Chicago.

2. **A:** _____ _____ you from?

   **B:** I'm from Tokyo in Japan.

3. **A:** Where are _____ _____ in Brazil?

   **B:** I'm from Curitiba.

4. **A:** Where are _____ _____ ?

   **B:** I'm _____ Australia.

5. **A:** _____ are you from in Korea?

   **B:** I'm _____ Seoul.

6. **A:** Where _____ you _____ ?

   **B:** _____ from Spain.

**5** Write questions and answers.

1.

You: _Where_ _are_ _you_ from in Italy?
Isabella: _I'm_ _from_ Rome.

2.

You: _____ _____ _____
_____ ?
Na: _____ _____ China.

3.

You: _____ _____ _____
_____ ?
Fabiana: _____ _____ Argentina.

4.

You: _____ _____ _____
_____ in Mexico?
Gael: _____ _____ Guadalajara.

# Communication

**6** Complete the conversation with the words from the box. Then complete the details.

> Pardon     from     ~~Hello~~     name
> Where     Nice to meet you, too

Stan: Hello.
Nadine: _Hello_ (**1**.).
Stan: I'm Stan Allman. What's your _____ (**2**.)?
Nadine: I'm Nadine Strong.
Stan: Nice to meet you, Nadine.
Nadine: _____ (**3**.), Stan.
Stan: This is Chris, Chris Hall.
Chris: Hello.
Nadine: Hello.
Stan: Where are you from, Nadine?
Nadine: _____ (**4**.)?
Stan: Where are you from?
Nadine: Oh. I'm from the US.
Stan: Oh really? _____ (**5**.) are you from in the US?
Nadine: Dallas. It's in Texas.
Stan: Chris is from the US.
Chris: No—I'm from Canada!
Stan: Oh, yes. Sorry.
Nadine: Where are you _____ (**6**.) in Canada, Chris?
Chris: Victoria. It's in British Columbia.
Nadine: Where are you from, Stan. Canada, too?
Stan: No—I'm from Cape Town in South Africa.
Nadine: Oh, OK. My mother is from South Africa.

7. Name: Stan _____
   From: _____ (city)
   From: _____ (country)

8. Name: Nadine _____
   From: _____ (city)
   From: _____ (country)

9. Name: Chris _____
   From: _____ (city)
   From: _____ (country)

# UNIT 2
# Family and friends

## LESSON 1

## Vocabulary

**1**   Look at the pictures. Complete the puzzle to find the secret word.

|   |   |   |   |   |   |   |   |
|---|---|---|---|---|---|---|---|
| 1 | P | H | O | N | E |   |   |

**2**   Look at the photo. How are the people related?

1. Homer – Bart = _father_ – _son_
2. Homer – Marge = _____ – _wife_
3. Lisa – Bart = _sister_ – _____
4. Marge – Lisa = _____ – _____
5. Bart – Marge = _____ – _____
6. Lisa – Homer = _____ – _____

**3**   Match the words to the numbers.

| _f_ | **1.** fifty-one | **a.** 93 |
|---|---|---|
| ____ | **2.** forty-eight | **b.** 15 |
| ____ | **3.** eleven | **c.** 73 |
| ____ | **4.** sixteen | **d.** 48 |
| ____ | **5.** ninety-three | **e.** 11 |
| ____ | **6.** seventy-three | **f.** 51 |
| ____ | **7.** fifteen | **g.** 84 |
| ____ | **8.** sixty | **h.** 39 |
| ____ | **9.** eighty-four | **i.** 60 |
| ____ | **10.** thirty-nine | **j.** 16 |

**4**   Write the next two numbers in the sequences.

1. two   four   eight   sixteen
   _thirty-two_   _sixty-four_
2. ninety   eighty   seventy   sixty
   _____   _____
3. eleven   twenty-two   thirty-three   forty-four
   _____   _____
4. sixteen   fifteen   fourteen   thirteen
   _____   _____
5. forty-nine   fifty-six   sixty-three   seventy
   _____   _____

# Grammar

**5**  Look at the family tree and complete the conversation.

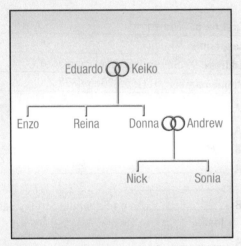

Eduardo ⚭ Keiko

Enzo    Reina    Donna ⚭ Andrew

Nick    Sonia

Ivan:  Nice photo!

Donna:  Thank you! It's a photo of my family.

Ivan:  _Who's_ (1.) he?

Donna:  He's my _____ (2.), Andrew. He's from the US.

Ivan:  New York?

Donna:  No, Los Angeles.

Ivan:  And who's _____ (3.) ?

Donna:  She's Reina. She's _____ (4.) sister. She's in Italy. And he's my _____ (5.), Eduardo. He's in Italy, too.

Ivan:  _____ (6.) he?

Donna:  He's Nick. He's my _____ (7.). And she's Sonia, _____ (8.) daughter.

Ivan:  _____ (9.) she?

Donna:  She's my _____ (10.), Keiko. She's from Japan.

Ivan:  An international family! Who's _____ (11.)?

Donna:  _____ (12.) Enzo, my brother.

# Reading

**6**  Read the descriptions. Then complete the details about the people.

**Who is Andy?**
Andy Branley is my friend. He's from San Diego in the US. He's thirty-five years old.

**Who is Darren?**
Darren is my father—Darren Southgate. He's fifty-seven. He's from Akron, Ohio in the US.

**Who is Beverley?**
Beverley Wolcott is my friend, too. She's from Dominica in the Caribbean. She's thirty-seven years old.

**Who is Pauline?**
Pauline Southgate is my mother. She's from York in the UK. She's sixty years old.

**Who are you?**
I'm David. I'm from Seattle in the US. I'm twenty-nine.

NAME: Darren Southgate
AGE: _57_
FROM: _Akron, Ohio_ in _the US_
RELATIONSHIP TO DAVID:
_father_

A

B

NAME: _____ _____
AGE: 35 years old
FROM: _____ in _____
RELATIONSHIP TO DAVID:
_____

NAME: _____ _____
AGE: _____
FROM: _____ in _____
RELATIONSHIP TO DAVID:
friend

C

D

NAME: _____ Southgate
AGE: _____
FROM: _____ in _____
RELATIONSHIP TO DAVID:
mother

# Vocabulary

**1** Match the words in the box to the pictures.

> bad  great  ~~good~~  awful  OK

1. ☺  *good*
2. ☹☹  _____
3. ☺☺  _____
4. 😐  _____
5. ☹  _____

**2** Write a sentence for each singer. Use the words from Exercise 1.

1. *She's good*  _____ .

2. _____ .

3. _____ .

4. _____ .

5. _____ .

# Grammar

**3** Read the information. Then complete the questions and answers.

> **First name:** Mario
> **Last name:** Vinicio
> **Address:** 93 Sabanilla Street, San José
> **Phone number:** 011-555-2366-4838

1. A: *What's your* _____ name?
   B: *My* _____ *name's* _____ Mario Vinicio.
2. A: _____ _____
   _____ ?
   B: _____ 93 Sabanilla Street, San José.
3. A: _____ _____
   _____ ?
   B: _____ 011-555-2366-4838.

**4** Write questions with *Who, What, Where,* or *How.*

1. *Who's she* _____ ?
   She's my friend.
2. _____ ?
   I'm 55.
3. _____ ?
   Jane Sutter.
4. _____ ?
   It's 323-555-5943.
5. _____ ?
   He's 19.
6. _____ ?
   Parson. P – A – R – S – O –N.
7. _____ ?
   I'm from Beijing, in China.
8. _____ ?
   75 Attley Street, Melbourne.
9. _____ ?
   Preston is my brother.
10. _____ ?
    She's from China.

**5** Correct the mistakes.

**Conversation A**

Receptionist: Good morning. Welcome ^to the Hatson Hotel. (**1.**)

Olivia: Thank you.

Receptionist: What your name, please? (**2.**)

Olivia: I Olivia Dukakis. (**3.**)

Receptionist: How you spell that? (**4.**)

Olivia: D – U – K – A – K – I – S.

Receptionist: Thank you, Ms. Dukakis. You in room 815. (**5.**)

**Conversation B**

Mr. Crowley: Hello.

Rick: Hello.

Mr. Crowley: What's name, please? (**1.**)

Rick: Rick Morley.

Mr. Crowley: How do you spell, please? (**2.**)

Rick: Morley. M – O – R – L – E – Y.

Mr. Crowley: What your address, Rick? (**3.**)

Rick: 81 Tavistock Street, Sydney.

Mr. Crowley: What do you spell Tavistock? (**4.**)

Rick: T – A – V – I – S – T – O – C – K.

Mr. Crowley: And what's your phone? (**5.**)

Rick: 208-555-3841.

## Writing

**6** Write the text messages.

1. _Are you from Brazil?_   2. _____

3. _____   4. _____

It's gr8!

C U later.

5. _____   6. _____

## Communication

**7** Read the conversation. Then complete the hotel form.

Woman: What's your name, please?

Man: I'm Brett Ellis.

Woman: How do you spell that?

Man: Brett. B – R – E – T – T. Ellis. E – L – L – I – S.

Woman: Thank you. What's your address?

Man: 33 Peel Street, Chappaqua.

Woman: How do you spell that, please?

Man: Peel Street. P – E – E – L. Chappaqua. C – H – A – P – P – A – Q – U – A.

Woman: And what's your phone number?

Man: Six – three – oh, five – five – five, two – one – four – nine.

First name: _____

Last name: _____

Address: _____

Phone number: _____

# Vocabulary

**1**   Complete the job words.

1. m _a_ n _a_ g _e_ r
2. t __ __ c h __ r
3. s t __ d __ n t
4. __ c c __ __ n t __ n t
5. s __ l __ s   c l __ r k
6. p __ l __ c __    __ f f __ c __ r
7. d __ c t __ r
8. __ r t __ s t
9. __ n g __ n __ __ r
10. __ c t __ r

**2**   Use the pictures to complete the puzzle.

**3**   Match the words to the answers.

_b_ 1. name
___ 2. occupation
___ 3. address
___ 4. age
___ 5. email address
___ 6. phone number

a. julia.mann@mail.net
b. ~~Julia Mann~~
c. engineer
d. 238-555-9653
e. 34
f. 12 King Street, Baltimore

# Grammar

**4**   Write sentences about each picture in Exercise 2. Use *a/an*.

1. *She's a doctor* .
2. _____ .
3. _____ .
4. _____ .
5. _____ .
6. _____ .
7. _____ .
8. _____ .
9. _____ .

**5**   Circle the correct word.

This is George Clooney. (*He's*)/*His* (**1.**) an actor. *He's*/*His* (**2.**) from the US. *He's*/*His* (**3.**) about 50 years old. *He's*/*His* (**4.**) friend is Brad Pitt. *He's*/*His* (**5.**) about 48 years old. *He's*/*His* (**6.**) an actor, too.

This is Michelle Douglas. *She's*/*Her* (**7.**) a sales clerk. *She's*/*Her* (**8.**) from Canada. *She's*/*Her* (**9.**) 26 years old. *She's*/*Her* (**10.**) husband is David Douglas. *He's*/*His* (**11.**) 27 years old. *He's*/*His* (**12.**) a doctor.

# Reading

**6** Complete the family tree with the names, ages, and occupations of the people.

## The Wallace family

He's Sam Wallace. His sister is Marie. He's forty-five years old, and he's an engineer. His wife is Monica.

She's Patricia Wallace. Her son is Sam. She's sixty-eight years old, and she's a teacher.

She's Debbie Wallace. Her mother is Monica. She's eleven years old, and she's a student.

He's Derek Wallace. His wife is Patricia and his daughter is Marie. He's sixty-five years old, and he's a doctor.

He's Trey Wallace. He's twelve years old, and he's a student. His father is Sam, and his mother is Monica.

She's Monica Wallace. Her husband is Sam. She's forty-four years old, and she's an accountant.

She's Marie Wallace. Her brother is Sam. She's thirty-eight years old, and she's a manager.

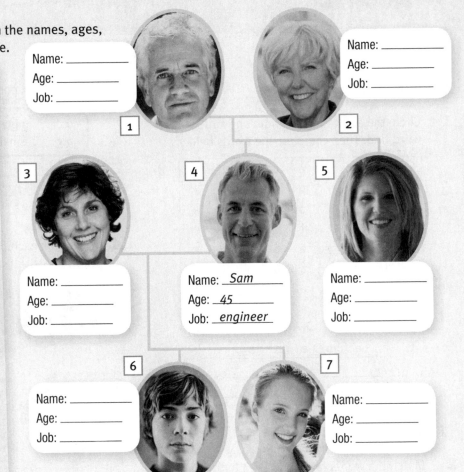

1 Name: _____ Age: _____ Job: _____

2 Name: _____ Age: _____ Job: _____

3 Name: _____ Age: _____ Job: _____

4 Name: _Sam_____ Age: _45_____ Job: _engineer_

5 Name: _____ Age: _____ Job: _____

6 Name: _____ Age: _____ Job: _____

7 Name: _____ Age: _____ Job: _____

**7** Complete the conversations.

1. A: What's __his____ (1.) name?
   B: _____ (2.) name's Rob Park.
   A: Where's _____ (3.) from?
   B: _____ (4.) from St. Louis.
   A: How old is _____ (5.)?
   B: _____ (6.) 55.
   A: What's _____ (7.) job?
   B: _____ (8.) a manager.
   A: What's _____ (9.) email address?
   B: _____ (10.) rpark@freemail.com.

2. A: What's _____ (11.) name?
   B: _____ (12.) name's Alva Braun.
   A: Where's _____ (13.) from?
   B: _____ (14.) from Toronto.
   A: How old is _____ (15.)?
   B: _____ (16.) 40 years old.
   A: What's _____ (17.) job?
   B: _____ (18.) an engineer.
   A: What's _____ (19.) cell phone number?
   B: _____ (20.) 416-555-0889.

# Vocabulary

**8** Write questions with *What's/Who's your favorite . . . ?* and the words from the box.

| book | ~~city~~ | CD |
| singer | movie | restaurant |

1. _What's your favorite city_____?
   Las Vegas.

2. _____?
   Gerrard's Bistro in Paris.

3. _____?
   Aretha Franklin.

4. _____?
   *Toy Story 3.*

5. _____?
   *Norwegian Wood* by Takashi Murakami.

6. _____?
   *Forty Licks* by the The Rolling Stones.

# UNIT **3**
# Traveling

LESSON **1**

## Vocabulary

**1** Circle the eight tourist attraction words in the word find. Then complete the words below.

| r | m | u | s | e | u | m | d | o |
|---|---|---|---|---|---|---|---|---|
| i | f | m | r | p | e | j | m | j |
| v | e | a | l | a | k | e | o | s |
| e | h | r | t | l | e | l | u | y |
| r | j | f | y | a | d | r | n | t |
| e | b | e | a | c | h | a | t | q |
| c | a | t | h | e | d | r | a | l |
| o | p | w | r | a | q | b | i | c |
| p | y | r | a | m | i | d | n | z |
| t | h | e | m | e | p | a | r | k |

1. ri *ver*_____   5. b_____
2. mo_____   6. t_____
3. py_____   7. p_____
4. mu_____   8. l_____

**2** Match the words from Exercise 1 to the pictures.

_____

_____

_____

_____

_____

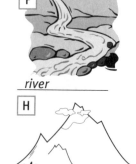
*river*
_____

G
_____

H
_____

**3** Write the opposite words from the box in pairs.

old     ugly     modern
big     small     beautiful

1. _____ – _____
2. _____ – _____
3. _____ – _____

**4** Describe each picture with two adjectives from Exercise 3.

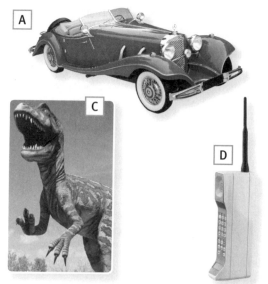

**A** The car is _*old*_____ and _*beautiful*_____.

**B** The camera is _____ and _____.

**C** The dinosaur is _____ and _____.

**D** The cell phone is _____ and _____.

**E** The television is _____ and _____.

16

# Grammar

**5** Circle the correct word.

1. My name is Kelly and his name is Larry. *(We're)/Our* from Liverpool in the UK.
2. *They're/Their* daughter is Lucy.
3. Richard and Julia are teachers. *They're/Their* my friends.
4. Carla is my sister. *We're/Our* mother is from Mexico.
5. Laura and Jill are in Kyoto in Japan. *They're/Their* in a hotel.
6. *We're/Our* car is very old.
7. What's *they're/their* email address?
8. Julian is a singer, but *we're/our* actors.

**6** Complete the email with *we're*, *they're*, *our*, or *their*.

From: rebeccaclark55@gmail.com
To: tomandsusan.clark@yahoo.com
Subject: We're in Recife!

Hi Mom and Dad,
How are you? Sarah and I are fine.
_We're_ (**1.**) in Recife in Brazil.
_____ (**2.**) hotel is great.
_____ (**3.**) in room 1111!
Belinda and Cipriano are in Recife, too.
_____ (**4.**) from São Paolo. They're
_____ (**5.**) friends.
The attachment is a photo of Belinda,
Cipriano, and Carlita in _____ (**6.**)
house in São Paolo. It's big! Carlita is
_____ (**7.**) daughter. She's beautiful.
Love,
Rebecca

**7** Complete the sentences with *we're*, *they're*, *our*, or *their*.

| The Jones family | The Watson family |

1. Mr. Watson: ___Their___ car is old.
   _____ car is modern.
2. Mr. Jones: _____ a big family.
   _____ a small family.
3. Mrs. Watson: _____ last name is Jones. _____ last name is Watson.
4. Mrs. Jones: _____ both 42 years old.
   _____ both 38 years old.
5. Mrs. Watson: _____ son is five.
   _____ children are 3, 6, 8, 12, and 16.

# Writing

**8** Put the email in order.

_____ **a.** The attachment is a picture of my sister and me in the Hotel Elise.

_____ **b.** See you soon!

_1_ **c.** From: lomox@patermail.com
To: josephine29@qwertymail.com
Subject: our vacation!

_____ **d.** Lola

_____ **e.** Thanks for your email. We're on vacation in Nice in France. Our hotel is the Hotel Elise. It's very small, but it's great. Nice is beautiful.

_____ **f.** Hi Josephine,

# Vocabulary

**1** Complete the words. Then match the words to the pictures.

| Words | Picture |
|---|---|
| 1. c _a_ _m_ _e_ _r_ _a_ | _D_ |
| 2. b _ _ _ _ _ _ | ___ |
| 3. b _ _ _ _ _ _ c _ | ___ |
| 4. _ _ _ _ of p _ _ _ s | ___ |
| 5. _ o o _ | ___ |
| 6. s _ _ _ r _ | ___ |
| 7. _ _ _ _ of s _ _ _ _ | ___ |
| 8. _ u _ t _ _ _ e | ___ |
| 9. m _ _ _ | ___ |
| 10. _ _ 3 p _ _ _ _ _ _ | ___ |

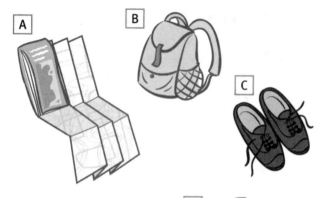

# Grammar

**2a** Write the names of the items in the picture.

| a. _two CDs_ | _/z/_ | f. _____ ___ |
| b. _____ ___ | | g. _____ ___ |
| c. _____ ___ | | h. _____ ___ |
| d. _____ ___ | | i. _____ ___ |
| e. _____ ___ | | j. _____ ___ |

**b** How does the "s" sound? Write /s/, /z/, or /ɪz/ next to the plural nouns in Exercise 2a.

**3** Rewrite the sentences. Make the underlined words plural.

1. My camera is in the suitcase.
   _Our cameras are in the suitcase_.

2. He's an accountant.
   _They're accountants_.

3. Where is my backpack?
   _____?

4. Who is your favorite singer?
   _____?

5. Her map is awful.
   _____.

6. It's a great MP3 player.
   _____.

7. My favorite pair of shoes is very old.
   _____.

8. How old is her daughter?
   _____?

**4** Use the cues to write negative sentences with the verb *be*.

1. He/my brother
   _He isn't my brother_ .

2. You/21 years old
   _____ .

3. It/my camera
   _____ .

4. Ronnie and Nicky/friends
   _____ .

5. Bogotá/my favorite city
   _____ .

6. We/students
   _____ .

7. I/a good actor
   _____ .

8. Simone/from Italy
   _____ .

9. Will and I/her teachers
   _____ .

10. I/very old
    _____ .

**5** Use the cues to correct the sentences.

1. A: I'm a teacher. (student)
   B: _You're not a teacher_ .
      _You're a student_ .

2. A: It's a skirt. (pair of pants)
   B: _____ .
      _____ .

3. A: We're from the US. (Canada)
   B: _____ .
      _____ .

4. A: Miami is my favorite city. (San José)
   B: _____ .
      _____ .

5. A: He's my sister. (brother)
   B: _____ .
      _____ .

6. A: I'm 15. (50)
   B: _____ .
      _____ .

7. A: They're open today. (closed)
   B: _____ .
      _____ .

8. A: She's an accountant. (engineer)
   B: _____ .
      _____ .

# Communication

**6a** Complete the conversation with the negative form of *be*. Use contractions.

| | |
|---|---|
| Teacher: | Good morning everyone. Where's the register? Ah, here it is. Three new students today! Who is Celia Cruz? |
| Celia: | I am. |
| Teacher: | Welcome to our English class, Celia. I'm Peter Keef: K – E – E – F. So, you're from Italy. |
| Celia: | No, _I'm not_ (1.) I'm from Spain. |
| Teacher: | Ah. Penelope Cruz is from Spain. She's your sister! |
| Celia: | No, no, she_____ (2.) my sister. She's from Madrid, and I_____ (3.) from Madrid. I'm from Valencia. |
| Teacher: | Oh, OK. And who are Raymond Petit and Catherine Petit? |
| Raymond: | We are. |
| Teacher: | You're brother and sister. |
| Catherine: | No, we _____ (4.). Raymond is my husband. |
| Raymond: | . . . and Catherine is my wife. |
| Teacher: | Wow! OK. You're married. Great. You're very young. How old are you? Twenty-three, twenty-four? |
| Raymond: | No, no. I'm twenty-nine, and Catherine is twenty-eight. |
| Teacher: | Oh, OK. Where are you from? |
| Catherine: | We're from Marseilles in France. |
| Raymond: | And how old are you, Mr Keef? Forty-five, forty-six? |
| Teacher: | No! I'm forty-one. |

**b** Mark each statement true (*T*) or false (*F*).

_F_ 1. The teacher is Peter Kuff.

_____ 2. Celia Cruz is the sister of Penelope Cruz.

_____ 3. Penelope Cruz is from Valencia in Spain.

_____ 4. Celia Cruz is from Valencia in Spain.

_____ 5. Raymond Petit is the brother of Catherine Petit.

_____ 6. Catherine and Raymond are from Marseilles in France.

_____ 7. Raymond is 29 years old.

_____ 8. Catherine is 24 years old.

_____ 9. The teacher is 46 years old.

**7** Correct the false sentences in Exercise 6b on a separate piece of paper.

1.
   The teacher is Peter Keef.

## Vocabulary

**1**  Complete the days of the week. Then put them in order.

___ W __ __ n __ __ day

___ Th __ __ __ day

___ F __ __ day

___ M __ __ day

___ S __ t __ __ day

___ T __ __ __ day

_1_ S _u_ _n_ day

**2**  Circle the correct sentence for each picture.

1.  a.  The mountain is here.
    **b.**  The mountain is there.

2.  a.  Here's your cell phone.
    b.  There's your cell phone.

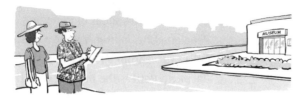

3.  a.  Here's the museum.
    b.  There's the museum.

4.  a.  Here are your shoes.
    b.  There are your shoes.

## Grammar

**3**  Complete the conversations. Then match them to the pictures below.

_____ **Conversation 1**

A:  Excuse me.

B:  Yes?

A:  _Are_ (**1.**) you from this town?

B:  Yes, we _____ (**2.**).

A:  Oh, good. _____ (**3.**) the museum near here?

B:  Yes, _____ (**4.**) is. It's over there.

A:  Thank you.

_____ **Conversation 2**

A:  _____ (**5.**) the movie theater big?

B:  Yes, it _____ (**6.**), madam. _____ (**7.**) very big.

A:  And _____ (**8.**) the movie good?

B:  It's very good. _____ (**9.**) they your sons?

A:  Yes, they _____ (**10.**).

B:  _____ (**11.**) _____ (**12.**) over 11 years old?

A:  No, they _____ (**13.**). They're 10 years old.

B:  Sorry madam. The movie is for children over 11 only.

_____ **Conversation 3**

A:  Hello, sir. _____ (**14.**) this your backpack?

B:  _____ (**15.**), it is.

A:  And _____ (**16.**) _____ (**17.**) your suitcases?

B:  Yes, _____ (**18.**) _____ (**19.**).

A:  What's your room number, sir?

B:  It's room 311.

A:  OK. Thank you, sir.

A

B

C

**4** Write questions with the adjectives in bold.

1. A: She's a singer.
   B: _Is she a good singer_____? **good**
   A: Yes, she is.
2. A: It's a museum.
   B: _____? **big**
   A: No, it isn't.
3. A: He's a friend.
   B: _____? **new**
   A: No, he isn't.
4. A: They're lakes.
   B: _____? **beautiful**
   A: Yes, they are.
5. A: I'm an actor.
   B: _____? **good**
   A: Yes, I am.
6. A: They're cities.
   B: _____? **small**
   A: No, they aren't.

**5** Look at the sign. Complete the conversation.

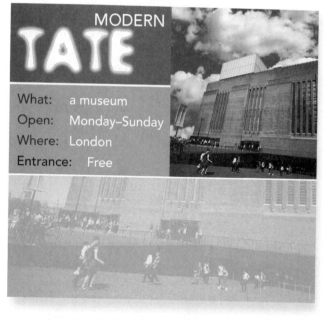

MODERN
**TATE**

What: a museum
Open: Monday–Sunday
Where: London
Entrance: Free

A: Good morning. Can I help you?
B: Yes. Is the Tate Modern _open___ (**1.**) today?
A: _____, _____ _____ (**2.**).
B: Good. _____ _____ (**3.**) a department store?
A: _____, _____ _____ (**4.**). It's a museum.
B: _____ _____ (**5.**) free?
A: _____, _____ _____ (**6.**).
B: _____ _____ (**7.**) near here?
A: Yes, _____ _____ (**8.**). Here's a map. We're here, and the Tate Modern is there.

# Reading

**6** Read the descriptions. Then match them to the pictures.

_____ **1.** Lake Baikal is a beautiful lake in Siberia, Russia. It is near Irkutsk, and it is very, very big. It is about 30 million years old.

_____ **2.** The New Museum of Contemporary Art is in New York in the US. It is not old (about 30 years old), but it is great. It is open from Tuesday to Sunday. Entrance is $6.

_____ **3.** The Golden Gate Bridge is in San Francisco in California. It is 75 years old. It is big and beautiful. It's open every day of the week. The toll is $6 for cars.

**7** Read the descriptions in Exercise 6 again and answer the questions.

**Lake Baikal**

1. Is Lake Baikal in Russia? _Yes, it is_____.
2. Is it near Siberia? _No, it isn't. It's in Siberia_.
3. Is it small? _____
4. Is it old? _____

**The Golden Gate Bridge**

5. Is the Golden Gate Bridge in San Francisco?
   _____
6. Is it new? _____
7. Is it open on Mondays? _____
8. Is it free? _____

**The New Museum of Contemporary Art**

9. Is it in the UK? _____
10. Is it old? _____
11. Is it closed on Mondays? _____
12. Is it free? _____

## Grammar
## Verb *be*

**1** Circle the correct word.

1. He *am/is/are* from Peru.
2. I *am/is/are* a student.
3. It *am/is/are* my car.
4. You *am/is/are* a good singer.
5. I *am/is/are* Mike.
6. Catherine *am/is/are* an accountant.
7. You *am/is/are* my friend.
8. She *am/is/are* my manager.
9. I *am/is/are* from China.
10. Tom *am/is/are* in Brazil.

**2** Rewrite the sentences using contractions.

1. She is Mrs. Grant.
   *She's Mrs. Grant* .

2. It is a great CD.
   _____ .

3. You are my favorite teacher.
   _____ .

4. I am Mr. Brown.
   _____ .

5. He is from New York.
   _____ .

6. Maria is a student.
   _____ .

**3** Write a negative sentence and a positive sentence with the cues.

1. (we/teachers/students)
   *We aren't teachers. We're students* .

2. (it/ugly/beautiful)
   *It's not ugly. It's beautiful* .

3. (she/from Spain/from Italy)
   _____ .

4. (Paul and Tom/great singers/awful singers)
   _____ .

5. (I/Mrs. Campbell/Miss Campbell)
   _____ .

6. (Joe/in the supermarket/in the museum)
   _____ .

7. (You/23 years old/24 years old)
   _____ .

## Possessive adjectives: *my/your/his/her/our/their*

**4** Complete the sentences with *my*, *your*, *his*, *her*, or *its*.

1. We are from Boston, but __*our*__ parents are from San Juan.
2. He's my father. __*His*__ name is Dave.
3. This is Moscow. _____ the capital of Russia.
4. I'm Yves. _____ last name is Connor.
5. Hello. What's _____ name?
6. Eleanor and John are our friends. _____ cat is named Cozy.
7. Jasmine is my friend. _____ email address is jasmine@xpressmail.net.
8. The waitress has two cups of cocoa. Is that _____ order?
9. _____ name is Julie. Nice to meet you.
10. I'm in an awful hotel. _____ name is the Hotel Riviera.
11. Miguel is an artist. _____ favorite movie is *The Godfather*.
12. You're my friend. _____ father is my friend, too.
13. Rachel is in Cambodia. _____ cell phone number is 806-21-447823.
14. Michael and Karen live on the beach. _____ house is beautiful.

## Questions

**5** Match the questions to the answers.

| | | |
|---|---|---|
| _j_ | 1. Where are you from? | a. It's in Ecuador. |
| ___ | 2. How old are you? | b. She's my manager. |
| ___ | 3. Who is she? | c. David. |
| ___ | 4. What is it? | d. It's a camera. |
| ___ | 5. Who are you? | e. I'm 49. |
| ___ | 6. Where is Porto Viejo? | f. He's my father. |
| ___ | 7. How old is he? | g. He's 19. |
| ___ | 8. What is his name? | h. I'm Martin Creek. |
| ___ | 9. What's your favorite movie? | i. *The Sting*. |
| ___ | 10. Who's he? | j. ~~Bangkok, Thailand~~. |

## Verb *to be*: Questions

**6**   Write questions and short answers with the cues.

1. A: (they/engineers) _Are they engineers_ ?
   B: (no) _No, they aren't_ .
2. A: (she/your sister) _____?
   B: (yes) _____.
3. A: (I/in room 515) _____?
   B: (no) _____.
4. A: (it/your favorite restaurant) _____?
   B: (yes) _____.
5. A: (we/in your class) _____?
   B: (no) _____.
6. A: (he/from Spain) _____?
   B: (yes) _____.
7. A: (you/Pedro) _____?
   B: (no) _____.
8. A: (Ivan and Vlad/brothers) _____?
   B: (yes) _____.

## Articles: *a/an*

**7**   Complete sentences with *a*, *an*, or nothing (–).

1. Natalie is in __–__ Colombia.
2. Jamie is _a_ sales clerk.
3. Emma is _____ actor.
4. What's your _____ email address?
5. It's _____ good movie.
6. Madrid is _____ great city.
7. She's from _____ China.
8. He's my _____ brother.
9. She's _____ accountant.
10. Who's your favorite _____ singer?

## Numbers 0–99

**8**   Match the numbers to the words.

| | | |
|---|---|---|
| _e_ | 1. 84 | a. nineteen |
| ___ | 2. 17 | b. seven |
| ___ | 3. 11 | c. fifteen |
| ___ | 4. 7 | d. eleven |
| ___ | 5. 50 | e. ~~eighty-four~~ |
| ___ | 6. 68 | f. seventeen |
| ___ | 7. 19 | g. twenty-three |
| ___ | 8. 70 | h. fifty |
| ___ | 9. 23 | i. seventy |
| ___ | 10. 15 | j. sixty-eight |

**9**   Write the numbers as words.

1. 25 _twenty-five_
2. 12 _____

3. 50 _____
4. 44 _____
5. 14 _____
6. 82 _____

## Vocabulary

**10**   Check (✓) the correct box.

| | Number | Job | Adjective | Family | Place |
|---|---|---|---|---|---|
| 1. manager | ☐ | ✓ | ☐ | ☐ | ☐ |
| 2. brother | ☐ | ☐ | ☐ | ☐ | ☐ |
| 3. awful | ☐ | ☐ | ☐ | ☐ | ☐ |
| 4. museun | ☐ | ☐ | ☐ | ☐ | ☐ |
| 5. good | ☐ | ☐ | ☐ | ☐ | ☐ |
| 6. eighty | ☐ | ☐ | ☐ | ☐ | ☐ |
| 7. accountant | ☐ | ☐ | ☐ | ☐ | ☐ |
| 8. eleven | ☐ | ☐ | ☐ | ☐ | ☐ |
| 9. son | ☐ | ☐ | ☐ | ☐ | ☐ |
| 10. palace | ☐ | ☐ | ☐ | ☐ | ☐ |
| 11. bad | ☐ | ☐ | ☐ | ☐ | ☐ |
| 12. engineer | ☐ | ☐ | ☐ | ☐ | ☐ |
| 13. fifty | ☐ | ☐ | ☐ | ☐ | ☐ |
| 14. wife | ☐ | ☐ | ☐ | ☐ | ☐ |

**11**   Complete the sentences with the words from the box.

| | | | |
|---|---|---|---|
| passport | Excuse | Friday | sixty |
| favorite | officer | clerk | map |
| suitcase | address | Nice | |
| website | ~~singer~~ | lake | |

1. My favorite _singer_ is Billie Holiday.
2. My _____ is 19 Lincoln Lane, Pittsburgh.
3. _____ me. Are you Derek?
4. We went to the museum on _____.
5. She's a great sales _____.
6. The photo in my _____ is very old.
7. Youtube.com is a great _____.
8. I packed my shoes in my _____.
9. My mother is _____ years old.
10. Is this your _____ CD?
11. We used a _____ to get to the beach.
12. _____ to meet you, too.
13. She's a police _____.
14. I went for a swim in the _____.

# UNIT 4
# Stores and restaurants

## LESSON 1

## Vocabulary

**1** Use the pictures to complete the puzzle.

1

2

3

4

5

6

7

8

**2** Complete the receipts for the trays of food.

1

CULTURE COFFEE SHOP RECEIPT
AUSTIN
**CUSTOMER COPY**
a. _coffee_ ............$1.09
b. _water_ ............$0.99
c. _____ ............$2.99
TOTAL............$5.07

2

PAULO'S RESTAURANT RECEIPT
BOSTON
**CUSTOMER COPY**
a. _____ ............$1.35
b. _____ ............$0.70
c. _____ ............$0.99
TOTAL............$3.04

3
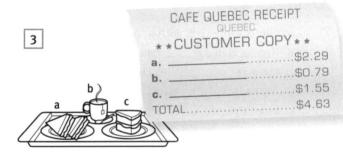

CAFE QUEBEC RECEIPT
QUEBEC
**CUSTOMER COPY**
a. _____ ............$2.29
b. _____ ............$0.79
c. _____ ............$1.55
TOTAL............$4.63

## Grammar

**3** Complete the conversations.

1. A: Hello. Can I _help_ (**1.**) you?
   B: Can I have _____ (**2.**) piece of cake and some bottled water, please?
   A: Certainly. Anything else?
   B: Yes. Can I have _____ (**3.**) cup of coffee?

2. A: Hello. _____ (**4.**) I help you?
   B: Yes. Can I _____ (**5.**) some coffee, some bottled water, and a chicken salad, please?
   A: Certainly. Anything else?
   B: No, _____ (**6.**) you.

3. A: Good morning.
   B: Good morning. Can I have _____ (**7.**) cheese sandwich and a piece of cake, please?
   A: Sure. Anything _____ (**8.**)?
   B: Yes. Can I have a cup of tea, _____ (**9.**)?
   A: Certainly.

24

## Vocabulary

**4a** Look at the cues. Correct the mistakes.

1. ($1.90) That's one euro ninety, please.
   _That's one dollar ninety, please_ .

2. ($2.54) That's two forty-five, please.
   _____ .

3. ($.50) That's fifty pence, please.
   _____ .

4. (£6.29) That's six euros and twenty-nine pence, please.
   _____ .

5. (€13.60) That's three euro sixty, please.
   _____ .

6. ($0.99) That's ninety-nine dollars, please.
   _____ .

7. ($11.49) That's eleven euros forty-nine, please.
   _____ .

8. (£90) That's eighty pounds, please.
   _____ .

**b** Look at the pictures. Complete the sentences.

1. The cell phone _is eighty-nine ninety-nine_ .
2. The CDs _____ .
3. The books _____ .
4. The camera _____ .
5. The pair of shoes _____ .
6. The backpack _____ .

## Communication

**5** Read the conversations. Then complete the menu board.

1. **A:** Good afternoon. Can I help you?
   **B:** Yes. Can I have a chicken salad sandwich and some bottled water, please?
   **A:** Sure. Anything else?
   **B:** Yes, please. An orange juice.
   **A:** OK, the chicken salad sandwich is two fifty and the bottled water is ninety cents. The orange juice is a dollar twenty, so that's four sixty, please.

2. **A:** Morning.
   **B:** Morning.
   **A:** What can I get you?
   **B:** Can I have coffee, a tea, and a house salad, please? To go.
   **A:** Sure. Anything else?
   **B:** No, thank you.
   **A:** OK, one coffee: That's one forty. One tea: That's one ninety-five. And one house salad: That's three dollars and ten cents. So altogether that's six forty-five.
   **B:** Here you are.
   **A:** Great. Thanks.

# MENU

## FOOD

| | |
|---|---|
| Chicken salad sandwich | _$2.50_ |
| House salad | _____ |

# DRINKS

| | |
|---|---|
| Orange juice | _____ |
| Bottled water | _____ |
| Coffee | _____ |
| Tea | _____ |

# Vocabulary

**1** Circle the eight color words in the word find. Then complete the words below.

| | | | | | |
|---|---|---|---|---|---|
| B | K | B | R | E | D |
| R | B | L | U | E | Y |
| O | R | A | N | G | E |
| W | P | C | D | R | L |
| N | Q | K | F | E | L |
| W | H | I | T | E | O |
| D | E | O | R | N | W |

1. b _r o w n_
2. w _ _ _ _
3. o _ _ _ _ _
4. g _ _ _ _
5. b _ _ _
6. b l _ _ _
7. y _ _ _ _ _ _
8. r _ _

**2** Look at the flags. What colors should they be?

1. Japan

_It's red and white_.

2. the UK

_____

3. Italy

_____

4. Turkey

_____

5. Egypt

_____

6. China

_____

7. Mexico

_____

8. Brazil

_____

**3** Look at the picture. Write the items of clothing.

1. _a hat_
2. _____
3. _____
4. _____
5. _____
6. _____
7. _____
8. _____

# Grammar

**4** Put the words in the correct order to make sentences.

1. are/white/These/nice/shirts
   _These white shirts are nice_ .

2. white/$24/bag/That/is
   _____ .

3. suitcase/your/Is/this
   _____ ?

4. those/Are/new/shirts
   _____ ?

5. closed/stores/today/are/These
   _____ .

6. Bob/This/my/is/brother,
   _____ .

7. are/Those/beautiful/bags
   _____ .

8. How/coat/much/that/is
   _____ ?

**5** Look at the picture. Circle the correct word.

1. (this)/*that/these/those* bag ($5.99)
2. *this/that/these/those* shirts ($10.99)
3. *this/that/these/those* T-shirts ($4.99)
4. *this/that/these/those* blouses ($15.99)
5. *this/that/these/those* hat ($4.50)
6. *this/that/these/those* coats ($77.99)
7. *this/that/these/those* skirts ($22.99)
8. *this/that/these/those* pairs of pants ($18.59)

## Communication

**6** Look at the picture in Exercise 5 again. Write the questions.

1. A: _How much are those shirts_ ?
   B: They're ten dollars and ninety-nine cents.
2. A: _____ ?
   B: They're four dollars and ninety-nine cents.
3. A: _____ ?
   B: It's four dollars and fifty cents.
4. A: _____ ?
   B: They're fifteen dollars and ninety-nine cents.
5. A: _____ ?
   B: They're seventy-seven dollars and ninety-nine cents.
6. A: _____ ?
   B: They're twenty-two dollars and ninety-nine cents.
7. A: _____ ?
   B: They're eighteen dollars and fifty-nine cents.
8. A: _____ ?
   B: It's five dollars and ninety-nine cents.

## Reading

**7** Read the story and answer the questions. Write complete sentences.

My name is Alfredo Mendez. I'm 24, and I'm from Mexico City. This is my clothing stall. It's also in Mexico City, on the San Jacinto Plaza. My stall is open from Monday to Saturday. The clothes are for men and women. For women I have dresses, skirts, shirts, shoes, and bags. Those red and pink dresses are very popular. They're 96 pesos—that's about 8 dollars. These skirts are very nice, too. They are yellow, blue, or pink. They're 60 pesos—that's about 5 dollars.

1. What is Alfredo's last name?
   _His last name is Mendez_ .
2. How old is he?
   _____ .
3. Where is he from?
   _____ .
4. Where is his market stall?
   _____ .
5. What is on sale at his market stall?
   _____ .
6. When is his market stall open?
   _____ .
7. How much are the dresses?
   _____ .
8. What color are the dresses?
   _____ .
9. How much are the skirts?
   _____ .
10. What color are the skirts?
   _____ .

# Vocabulary

**1**   Write the plural form of the words.

1. One child. Two __children__ .
2. One woman. Two _____ .
3. One man. Two _____ .
4. One baby. Two _____ .
5. One person. Two _____ .
6. One wife. Two _____ .

# Grammar

**2**   Look at the chart. Then use the cues to write sentences.

|  | Silvia | Julian | Petra | Mr. Webber |
|---|---|---|---|---|
| House | new | old | big | small |
| Children | 7, 8, and 9 years old | 12 and 14 years old | 3 and 6 years old | 2 and 3 years old |
| Car | red | blue | green | yellow |
| Parents | from Paraguay | from the UK | from Russia | from the US |

1. (Julian/car) _Julian's car is blue_ .
2. (Mr. Webber/children) _Mr. Webber's_ _children are two and three years old_ .
3. (Silvia/house) _____ .
4. (Petra/parents) _____ .
5. (Mr. Webber/house) _____ .
6. (Julian/children) _____ .
7. (Petra/car) _____ .
8. (Silvia/parents) _____ .
9. (Julian/house) _____ .
10. (Petra/children) _____ .
11. (Silvia/car) _____ .
12. (Julian/parents) _____ .

**3**   Look at the chart in Exercise 2 again. Write questions using the words in **bold**.

1. _Is Silvia's car blue_ ? **blue**
   No, it isn't. It's red.
2. _____ ? **2 and 5 years old**
   No, they aren't. They're three and six years old.
3. _____ ? **from the US**
   No, they aren't. They're from the UK.
4. _____ ? **big**
   No, it isn't. It's small.
5. _____ ? **from Russia**
   No, they aren't. They're from Paraguay.

6. _____ ? **blue**
   No, it isn't. It's green.
7. _____ ? **new**
   No, it isn't. It's old.
8. _____ ? **12 and 14 years old**
   No, they aren't. They're two and three years old.

**4**   Look at the pictures. Answer the questions.

Julio

Mei

Arabella

Armand

Giacomo

Larisa

1. Are they Julio's shoes?
   _No, they aren't_ . _They're Arabella's shoes_ .
2. Is it Giacomo's coffee?
   _____ . _____ .
3. Are they Ting's children?
   _____ . _____ .
4. Is it Larisa's hat?
   _____ . _____ .
5. Are they Armand's books?
   _____ . _____ .
6. Is it Arabella's orange juice?
   _____ . _____ .

**5** Read the sentences. What is the meaning of *'s*? Write P (possessive *'s*) or I (*is*).

<u>_I_</u> **1.** Amado's my brother.

_____ **2.** Blanca's brother is Claudio.

_____ **3.** Where is Keiko's bag?

_____ **4.** Johann's not here today.

_____ **5.** Who is Hilda's friend?

_____ **6.** Jake's camera is great.

_____ **7.** Karla's my friend.

_____ **8.** Is Suzanne's last name Webber?

# Communication

**6** Complete the conversations with the words from the box.

> pay by credit card     Sign
> PIN number     Can I
> ~~One-way or round-trip~~     That's

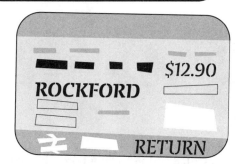

A: Can I help you?

B: Yes. Can I have a ticket to Rockford, please?

A: <u>_One-way or round-trip_</u> (**1.**)?

B: Round-trip please.

A: That's $12.90, please.

B: Can I _____ (**2.**)?

A: Yes. _____ (**3.**) here, please. Thank you.

B: Thank you.

C: Can I help you?

D: Yes. Can I have a ticket to *Monsters 5*, please?

C: _____ (**4.**) $7.50, please.

D: _____ (**5.**) pay by credit card?

C: Certainly. Enter your _____ (**6.**), please. Thank you.

D: Thank you.

**7a** Complete the conversations with *Can* and *please*. Then match the conversations to the pictures.

> _____ **Conversation 1**
>
> A: <u>_Can_</u> (**1.**) I help you?
>
> B: Yes. _____ (**2.**) I have two tickets for the new Johnny Depp movie, _____ (**3.**)?
>
> A: *Red Train?*
>
> B: Yes, that's it.
>
> A: Two adults?
>
> B: No. One adult and one child, _____ (**4.**).
>
> A: OK, that's fifteen fifty.
>
> B: _____ (**5.**) I pay by credit card?
>
> A: Certainly.
>
> _____ **Conversation 2**
>
> A: Good morning.
>
> B: Good morning. _____ (**6.**) I have a round-trip ticket to Bridgeport, please?
>
> A: Just one person?
>
> B: Yes.
>
> A: That's eighteen dollars and ten cents, _____ (**7.**).
>
> B: _____ (**8.**) I pay by credit card?
>
> A: Of course.

Ticket: *to Brighton* / *to Bridgeport*
People: *one person* / *two people*
Price: *$18.10* / *$80.10*

Movie: *Red Train* / *Red Ten*
People: *1 adult and 1 child* / *2 adults*
Tickets: *$15.50* / *$16.50*

**b** Circle the correct words below each picture.

# Things to see and do

## Vocabulary

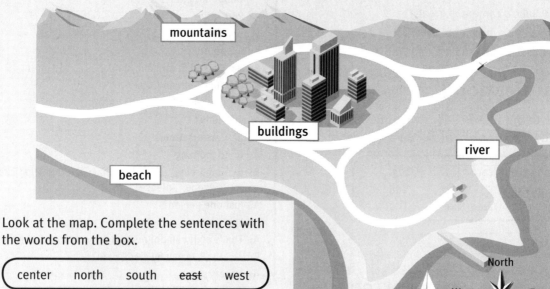

**1** Look at the map. Complete the sentences with the words from the box.

> center    north    south    ~~east~~    west

1. The river is _east_____ of the city.
2. The buildings are in the _____ of the city.
3. The mountains are _____ of the city.
4. The beach is _____ and _____ of the city

## Communication

**2** Put the words in the correct order to make sentences.

1. is/think/this/beautiful/I/beach
   _I think this beach is beautiful_____.

2. city/I/New York/great/think/a/is
   _____.

3. think/those/I/ugly/buildings/are
   _____.

4. don't/manager/a/Francis/is/think/good/I
   _____.

5. beautiful/countryside/think/important/a/good/vacation/I/for/is
   _____.

## Grammar

**3** Complete the brochure on the right with *there's* or *there are*.

### A Quick Guide to Five English Towns

**Brighton**

Brighton is only one hour from London.
_There's_____ (**1.**) a beach near the center of town, and _____ (**2.**) small stores and coffee shops in Brighton.

**Canterbury**

_____ (**3.**) great shopping in Canterbury, and _____ (**4.**) a beautiful river: the River Stour.

**Nottingham**

_____ (**5.**) good restaurants in Nottingham, and _____ (**6.**) great tourist attractions near the center of town.

**York**

York is very old, and _____ (**7.**) 600-year-old streets in the town. _____ (**8.**) also beautiful buildings.

**Bristol**

Bristol is in the west of England. _____ (**9.**) a beautiful bridge: the Clifton Suspension Bridge. _____ (**10.**) also great museums.

**4** Look at the website. Write sentences with *There's* or *There are*.

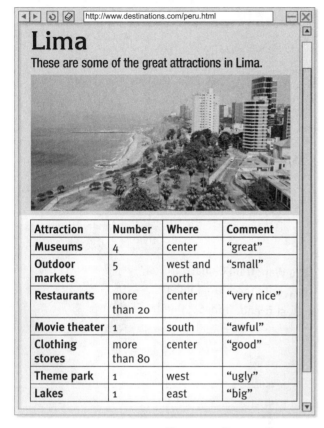

http://www.destinations.com/peru.html

# Lima
These are some of the great attractions in Lima.

| Attraction | Number | Where | Comment |
|---|---|---|---|
| Museums | 4 | center | "great" |
| Outdoor markets | 5 | west and north | "small" |
| Restaurants | more than 20 | center | "very nice" |
| Movie theater | 1 | south | "awful" |
| Clothing stores | more than 80 | center | "good" |
| Theme park | 1 | west | "ugly" |
| Lakes | 1 | east | "big" |

1. (outdoor markets) *There are five small outdoor markets in the west and north of Lima*.
2. (museums) _____.
3. (clothing stores) _____.
4. (movie theaters) _____.
5. (restaurants) _____.
6. (lakes) _____.
7. (theme park) _____.

## Vocabulary

**5** Rewrite the sentences in Exercise 4 with *a/an*, *some*, or *a lot of*.

1. *There are some small outdoor markets in the west and north of Lima*.
2. _____.
3. _____.
4. _____.
5. _____.
6. _____.
7. _____.

## Reading

**6** Read about three language schools in the US. Then complete the chart.

http://www.USlanguageSchools.com

# Language Schools

### Name: The Bay Area School of English

The Bay Area School of English is in San Francisco. There are 14 classrooms and a cafeteria for students. There is an Internet café with ten computers. San Francisco is on the west coast. It's a great city, and there are a lot of restaurants, stores, and coffee shops. The big tourist attractions are the Golden Gate Bridge and Alcatraz.

### Name: NYC English School

The NYC English School is in the center of New York City, on the east coast of the US. There are 25 classrooms, and the classes are small—between seven and ten students. There is an Internet café next to the school, and there is a movie theater and a shopping center near the school. The big tourist attractions are Central Park, the museums, and the East Village.

### Name: Chicago School of English

The Chicago School of English is in downtown Chicago. There are 15 classrooms and 30 teachers. There are two Internet cafés and a TV room for students. Chicago is in the center of the US. The shopping and museums in Chicago are great, but the big tourist attractions are outdoor activities on Lake Michigan, the theme park, and the zoo.

|  | The Bay Area School of English | NYC English School | Chicago School of English |
|---|---|---|---|
| City | San Francisco |  |  |
| Where |  | the east coast of the US |  |
| Classrooms |  |  |  |
| Internet café |  |  |  |
| Big tourist attractions |  |  |  |

# Vocabulary

**1** Circle eight prepositions of place (one, two, or three words) in the word find.

| x | y | t | p | k | z | r | o | a |
|---|---|---|---|---|---|---|---|---|
| i | a | g | b | u | r | f | s | c |
| n | e | x | t | t | o | d | u | r |
| f | x | u | n | l | o | o | r | o |
| r | c | o | n | z | a | h | d | s |
| o | p | p | o | s | i | t | e | s |
| n | m | p | j | s | n | y | n | f |
| t | q | n | e | a | r | u | h | r |
| o | a | l | k | d | g | m | b | o |
| f | d | b | e | h | i | n | d | m |

**2** Look at the picture. Complete the sentences with words from the box.

> behind    in front of    across from
> near      next to        ~~in~~

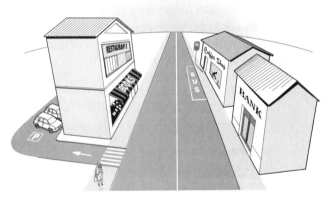

1. The man is ___in___ the coffee shop.
2. The coffee shop is _____ the bookstore.
3. The bus stop is _____ the coffee shop.
4. The parking lot is _____ the bookstore.
5. The bank is _____ the coffee shop.
6. The woman is _____ the bookstore.

**3** Read the information. Write sentences about the people.

> **Pierre:** from France
> **Favorite food:** from Italy
> **Car:** from Japan

1. _Pierre's French_ .
2. _His favorite food is Italian_ .
3. _His car is Japanese_ .

> **Yu Wan:** from China
> **Favorite food:** from India
> **Best friend:** from Scotland

4. _____ .
5. _____ .
6. _____ .

> **Angela:** from Germany
> **Favorite food:** from Russia
> **Husband:** from Brazil

7. _____ .
8. _____ .
9. _____ .

> **Jay:** from US
> **Favorite food:** from Thailand
> **Wife:** from Australia

10. _____ .
11. _____ .
12. _____ .

# Grammar

**4** Look at the shopping center plan. Complete the questions and answers.

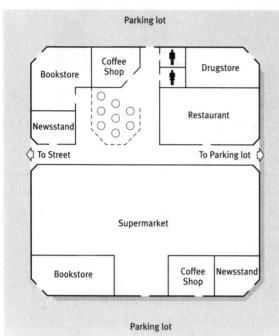

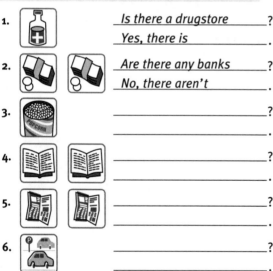

1. *Is there a drugstore* ?
   *Yes, there is* .

2. *Are there any banks* ?
   *No, there aren't* .

3. _____ ?
   _____ .

4. _____ ?
   _____ .

5. _____ ?
   _____ .

6. _____ ?
   _____ .

**5** Write affirmative or negative sentences about the shopping center in Exercise 4. Use the cues.

1. (parking lot) *There's a parking lot* .
2. (shoe stores) *There aren't any shoe stores* .
3. (restaurant) _____ .
4. (supermarket) _____ .
5. (department stores) _____ .
6. (train station) _____ .
7. (bookstores) _____ .
8. (museums) _____ .
9. (bank) _____ .
10. (movie theaters) _____ .

# Reading

**6** Read the conversation. Then complete the map.

A: Is there a hotel near here?

B: Yes, there are two. There's a big hotel across from the train station, and there's a very nice hotel next to the movie theater on Venice Road.

A: Great, thanks. Are there museums here?

B: No, there aren't.

A: Is there a drugstore?

B: Yes, there is. There's one across from the supermarket.

A: Great. Is there a coffee shop?

B: Yes, there are two. There's a coffee shop on Carnival Street, next to the supermarket, and there's a coffee shop across from the movie theater.

A: Thank you!

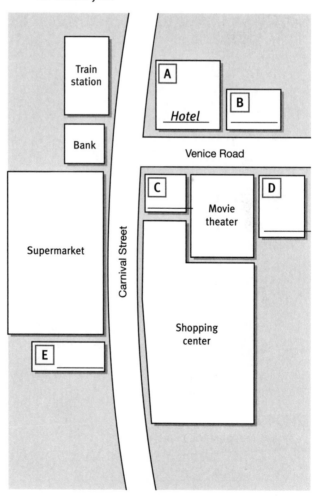

# Vocabulary

**1** Write a verb or phrase for each picture.

1.  _dance_

2.  _____

3.  _____

4.  _____

5.  _____

6. 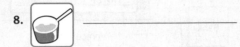 _____

7. _____

8. _____

# Grammar

**2** Use cues to write sentences with *can* and *can't*.

1. (I/sing ✔)
   _I can sing but I can't play the_
   _piano_ .

2. (Jim and Jane/drive ✗)
   _____
   _____ .

3. (Loretta/swim ✗)
   _____
   _____ .

4. (You/play the piano ✔)
   _____
   _____ .

5. (Sebastian/dance ✗)
   _____
   _____ .

6. (You and I/sing ✗)
   _____
   _____ .

**3** Complete the conversation with the phrases from the box.

| He can | I can | I can't | Can you speak |
|--------|-------|---------|----------------|
| Can he | can | ~~can you~~ | They can |

A: So, Mrs. Redwood, _can you_ (1.) speak Italian?

B: Yes, _____ (2.). My mother and father are from Italy. _____ (3.) speak Italian, English, French, and Spanish.

A: Great. _____ (4.) French and Spanish?

B: I _____ (5.) speak Spanish but _____ (6.) speak French.

A: That's OK. Mr. Ploton is the manager. _____ (7.) speak French.

B: _____ (8.) speak English?

A: No, he can't.

**4** Look at the chart. Use the cues to complete the sentences.

| | Jo | Simon | Leroy and Lena |
|---|----|-------|----------------|
| speak Spanish | ✓ | ✗ | ✗ |
| drive | ✗ | ✗ | ✓ |
| use a computer | ✗ | ✓ | ✓ |

1. (Leroy and Lena/use a computer)
   Leroy and Lena _can use a computer_ .

2. (Jo/use a computer) Jo _can't use a computer_ .

3. (Simon/drive)
   A: _Can Simon drive_ ?
   B: _No, he can't_ .

4. (Leroy and Lena/speak Spanish)
   _____ .

5. (Jo/speak Spanish)
   A: _____ ?
   B: _____ .

6. (Simon/use a computer) _____ .

7. (Leroy and Lena/drive)
   A: _____ ?
   B: _____ .

8. (Jo/drive) _____ .

9. (Simon/drive) _____ .

# Communication

**5** Today is Linda's first day in her new job. Read the conversation. Then complete the map of the office with the words in the box.

> A: Welcome to North-South Travel.
> B: Thank you.
> A: I'm Edward Cole, your new manager.
> B: Nice to meet you, Mr. Cole.
> A: Nice to meet you, too, Linda. What's your last name?
> B: Brown.
> A: OK. Well, please, call me Edward. So, it's your first day!
> B: That's right.
> A: Well, this is your desk. There's a computer and a telephone. My desk is here, in front of your desk. Can you use a computer?
> B: Yes, I can.
> A: Great. Now, our main office is in Colombia. Can you speak Spanish?
> B: Yes, I can.
> A: Good. And can you speak Italian? Some of our customers are from Italy.
> B: No, I can't. But I can speak French.
> A: Oh, that's great. I can speak Italian, but I can't speak Spanish. That's Rachel's desk over there, next to the window, and Darren's desk is over there, behind the plants.
> B: Who's Darren?
> A: Oh, he's our accountant. He's great . . .

| Linda's desk | ~~Edward's desk~~ |
| Rachel's desk | Darren's desk |

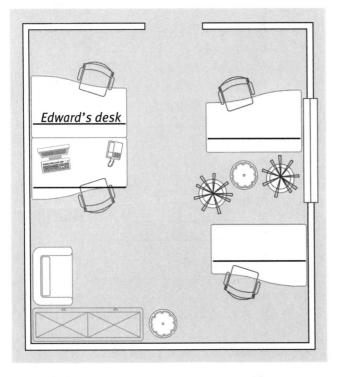

Edward's desk

# 6 Make sentences about Edward and Linda using *can*.

1. Linda/use a computer
   *She can use a computer* .
2. Edward/speak Italian
   _____ .
3. Linda/speak Spanish
   _____ .
4. Linda/speak French
   _____ .
5. Linda/speak Italian
   _____ .
6. Edward/speak Spanish
   _____ .

# Vocabulary

**7** Write the times next to the clocks.

1. `10:00` *ten o'clock*

2.  *four forty-five*

3. `06:30` _____

4. `09:50` _____

5. `11:20` _____

6. `01:00` _____

7. `08:30` _____

8. `06:15` _____

9. `05:35` _____

10. `05:05` _____

# UNIT 6
# All about you

## LESSON 1

## Vocabulary

**1a** Circle five adjectives in the word find. Then complete the words below.

| s | h | o | r | t |
|---|---|---|---|---|
| b | s | a | i | h |
| o | l | d | c | i |
| m | l | u | h | n |
| h | a | p | p | y |

1. s _h_ _o_ _r_ _t_     3. o _ _     5. t _ _ _
2. r _ _ _     4. h _ _ _ _

**b** Write the opposite words.

1. tall _____     4. poor _____
2. unhappy _____     5. young _____
3. heavy _____

**2** Label the pictures with adjectives from Exercise 1.

1  *short*

2  _____

3  _____

4  _____

5  _____

6  _____

7  _____

8  _____

9  _____

10  _____

## Grammar

**3a** Use the cues to make sentences with *I like* or *I don't like*.

1. (☺/coffee)
   _I like coffee_ .
2. (☹/museums)
   _I don't like museums_ .
3. (☺/rap music)
   _____ .
4. (☹/soccer)
   _____ .
5. (☺/computers)
   _____ .
6. (☹/Indian food)
   _____ .
7. (☹/tea)
   _____ .
8. (☺/children)
   _____ .
9. (☺/James Bond films)
   _____ .
10. (☹/my manager)
    _____ .

**b** Write questions and answers about the words in **bold**.

1. A: _Do you like coffee_ ? **coffee**
   B: Yes, _I do_ .
2. A: _Do you like the countryside_ ? **the countryside**
   B: No, _I don't_ .
3. A: _____ ? **Chinese food**
   B: Yes, _____ .
4. A: _____ ? **modern buildings**
   B: No, _____ .
5. A: _____ ? **salad**
   B: Yes, _____ .
6. A: _____ ? **German cars**
   B: No, _____ .
7. A: _____ ? **Harry Potter**
   B: Yes, _____ .
8. A: _____ ? **The Beatles**
   B: No, _____ .

36

# Grammar

**4a** Replace the <u>underlined</u> words with object pronouns: *me, you, him, her, it, us,* or *them.*

## Now that I'm 70 . . .
by Harold Parks

Now that I'm 70, I am happy. I have a lot of best friends. My children are my best friends. I like <u>my children</u> (**1.**). My sister is my best friend—I like <u>my sister</u> (**2.**). My brother is my best friend. I like <u>my brother</u> (**3.**). The television is my best friend. We are together every evening. I like <u>the television</u> (**4.**). And you are my best friend. I like <u>you</u> (**5.**). Do you like <u>Harold Parks</u> (**6.**)?

1. _____*them*_____
2. _____
3. _____
4. _____
5. _____
6. _____

**b** Replace the <u>underlined</u> words with the object pronouns or subject pronouns.

1. <u>You and</u> I are rich. _____*We*_____
2. They like <u>you and me</u>. _____
3. <u>Kevin and Carrie</u> are engineers. _____
4. Do you like <u>Kevin and Carrie</u>? _____
5. <u>Ella Fitzgerald</u> is my favorite singer. _____
6. I like <u>Ella Fitzgerald</u>. _____
7. <u>Richard</u> is my best friend. _____
8. I like <u>Richard</u>. _____

# Reading

**5** Read the answers. Match the questions from the box to the answers. One question will be used twice.

> Do you like big cities?
> Do you like vacations on the coast?
> Who are your favorite actors?
> What are your favorite things in life?
> Do you like pop music?

**1.** <u>*Do you like pop music?*</u>
Yes, I do—some of it. I like Christina Aguilera and Katie Perry—they're great.

**2.** _____
That's easy: Javier Bardem, Halle Berry, and Susan Sarandon. Javier Bardem is great in *Biutiful*. It's a really good film.

Kimberley

Micaela

**3.** _____
Yes, I do. Paris, Buenos Aires, and Kyoto are my favorites. Buenos Aires is fantastic.

**4.** _____
I like French films, chocolate, coffee from Africa, the color brown, and Italian fashion, for example, Versace.

**5.** _____
No, I don't, but I like vacations in the countryside. I think beach vacations are awful, but a vacation in, for example, the Rocky Mountains in the US, now that's great.

**6.** _____
That's a good question. I like Sunday mornings in bed, my friends, and family and . . . a good book.

Peter

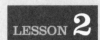

## Vocabulary

**1** Look at the pictures. Complete the sentences.

1. Fashion ___designers___ design clothes.

2. _____ cook food.

3. _____ build buildings.

4. _____ sell things.

5. _____ write articles.

6. _____ design buildings.

## Grammar

**2** Look at the chart. Complete Grace's sentences.

|  | Grace and Marlon | Steve and Shena |
|---|---|---|
| 1. like their job | YES | NO |
| 2. work in an office | YES | NO |
| 3. sell cars | NO | YES |
| 4. design buildings | YES | NO |

1. Grace: _We like our jobs_ .    3. Grace: _____ .
   _They don't like their jobs_ .          _____ .

2. Grace: _____ .    4. Grace: _____ .
   _____ .              _____ .

**3** Look at the magazine pictures. Complete the interview.

### WEEKEND HOUSE SWAP

Two couples swap houses for a weekend and decorate!

**Reporter:** So, Sara and Mark, what do you
         ___do___ (1.)?

**Sara:** _____ (2.) fashion designers.

**Reporter:** And what about Pete and Nancy. What
         _____ (3.) they do?

**Mark:** _____ (4.) sales reps.

**Reporter:** What do Pete and Nancy _____ (5.)?

**Sara:** They like the coast and the countryside.
_____ (6.) like blues and greens in
their house. They like boats and rivers, but they
_____ (7.) like cities, and they don't
_____ (8.) black.

**Reporter:** _____ (9.) do you like? Do
_____ (10.) like blues and greens in your
house?

**Mark:** No, we _____ (11.). We like white. We
like cities and towns. We _____ (12.)
the countryside and the coast, too, but just for a
weekend.

**Reporter:** OK, thanks. Happy decorating!

**4a** Complete the questions.

1. What _____*do*_____ you design?
2. _____ do you do?
3. Where _____ you live?
4. _____ do you work for?
5. _____ do you work?

**b** Complete the conversation with the questions from Exercise 4a.

**Neil:** Excuse me. Kate, this is Lance.

**Kate:** Hello, Lance. Nice to meet you.

**Lance:** Nice to meet you, too.

**Kate:** _What do you do_ (1.)?

**Lance:** I'm a fashion designer.

**Kate:** Oh really? _____ (2.)?

**Lance:** It's a company called Confident Designs.

**Kate:** _____ (3.)?

**Lance:** I design shoes and clothes.

**Kate:** Great! _____ (4.)?

**Lance:** In a small office in Brooklyn.

**Kate:** _____ (5.)?

**Lance:** In a house on Long Island. What do you do?

# Communication

**5a** Complete the conversation with the words from the box.

| articles | do | ~~Great!~~ | Oh really? |
|---|---|---|---|
| Where | Who | What | sales rep |

**Jose:** How is your food?

**Marta:** _Great!_ (1.) And this restaurant is beautiful.

**Jose:** Thanks. And you, sir?

**Ricardo:** Great, thank you. _____ (2.) is the chef?

**Jose:** I am.

**Ricardo:** _____ (3.)

**Jose:** Really. I'm glad you like the food. . . . Is this your first time in New York?

**Ricardo:** No, no. My wife and I come here a lot, for work.

**Jose:** _____ (4.) do you do?

**Marta:** I'm a _____ (5.) for a coffee machine company. I sell machines to restaurants and coffee shops—those kinds of places. And my husband is a reporter.

**Ricardo:** I write travel _____ (6.) for magazines—about US vacation places.

**Jose:** _____ (7.) do you live?

**Marta:** In Miami, Florida. What about you—Where _____ (8.) you come from?

**Jose:** Brazil. But now New York is my home.

**b** What are the people's occupations?

Jose: _____

Ricardo: _____

Marta: _____

# Vocabulary

**1a** Match the verbs to the nouns. One noun will be used more than once.

_d_ 1. watch    **a.** to bed
____ 2. start    **b.** up
____ 3. eat    **c.** work
____ 4. finish    ~~**d.** TV~~
____ 5. go    **e.** shower
____ 6. get    **f.** a sandwich
____ 7. take a

**b** Match the phrases in Exercise 1a to the pictures.

1 _get up_     2 _____

4 _____

3 _____

5 _____

6 _____

7 _____

# Grammar

**2** Look at the pictures in Exercise 1b. Write sentences.

1. _She gets up at 10:30_ .
2. _____ .
3. _____ .
4. _____ .
5. _____ .
6. _____ .
7. _____ .

**3** Read the description. Answer the questions.

1. Does Mrs. Moody start work early?
   _Yes, she does_ .

2. Does she eat breakfast?
   _____ .

3. Does she drink coffee?
   _____ .

4. Does she go to the restaurant for lunch?
   _____ .

5. Does she finish work late?
   _____ .

6. Does she have any friends?
   _____ .

My manager is Mrs. Moody. She starts work at seven o'clock every morning. She doesn't eat breakfast. She has a coffee at eleven o'clock. She has salad for lunch. She doesn't go to a restaurant—she eats her salad at her desk. She finishes work at about eight o'clock. She doesn't have any friends.

**4** Use the cues to write complete sentences.

1. (I/like/salad)
   _I like salad_ .

2. (Cheryl/finish/her English class/ten thirty)
   _Cheryl finishes her English class at ten thirty_ .

3. (They/work/in a restaurant)
   _____ .

4. (Hilary and Ben/not/eat fast food)
   _____ .

5. (Connor/not/eat salad)
   _____ .

6. (you/go to bed early?)
   _____ .

7. (Uma/like/me?)
   _____ .

8. (What/she/do?)
   _____ .

## Communication

**5** Read Ina's story. Then complete the chart.
✓ = like/love; ✗ = don't/doesn't like.

|  | Ina | Billy | Bianca | Larry and Mel |
|---|---|---|---|---|
| Ina |  | ✓ |  |  |
| Billy |  |  |  |  |
| Bianca |  |  |  |  |
| Larry and Mel |  |  |  |  |

Ina

So . . . my family is a bit strange. There's my husband, Billy, my best friend, Bianca, and my parents, Larry and Mel. Now I love Billy, of course, and Billy loves me. But Billy doesn't like Bianca. I don't know why, but he doesn't. And Bianca doesn't like him. She likes my parents, and they like her, but they don't like Billy. And, you know what, Billy doesn't like them. Now, of course, I like Bianca and my parents, and they all like me. But Billy isn't popular.

## Writing

**6** Complete the letter with the phrases from the box.

> How are you?
> and my team likes me.
> ~~89 Oak Street,~~
> Dear Stephen,
> Please write and tell me your news.
> Best wishes,
> December 2

Apartment 15
_89 Oak Street_ (1.)
Cleveland, OH

_____ (2.)

_____ (3.)

_____ (4.) I hope you're well.

I have a new job: I'm still with Copy Fast, but I'm a manager now. I get up early, and I work late. But I like my job _____ (5.).

David, the old manager, is a sales rep now. He works for a small company. He doesn't like his new job. He starts work early, and he drives all over the country.

_____ (6.)

_____ (7.)

Gary

## There is/are

**1** Complete the conversation with *there's, there is, there isn't, there are, there aren't, Is there,* or *Are there.*

1. A: Good morning. _Is there_ (**1.**) a bank near here?

   B: Yes, _____ (**2.**). It's on Parliament Street.

   A: And _____ (**3.**) any museums near here?

   B: Yes, _____ (**4.**).
   _____ (**5.**) a small museum on Baker Street, and _____ (**6.**) a big museum across from the train station.

2. C: Hello. _____ (**7.**) any good restaurants in town?

   D: Yes, _____ (**8.**).
   _____ (**9.**) a good Japanese restaurant on Gatson Street, and
   _____ (**10.**) two good Mexican restaurants on Mile Road.

   C: Great. And _____ (**11.**) an ATM in this hotel?

   D: No, _____ (**12.**).

## this/that/these/those

**2** Circle the correct word.

1. *Those/(This)/These* is my brother.
2. Who are *that/this/those* people over there?
3. How much is *that/these/those* hat?
4. Is *this/those/these* your camera?
5. *That/These/This* are my favorite stores.
6. This blue skirt is $19.99, and *those/that/this* red skirts are $21.99.
7. Can I have *those/these/that* white bag, please?
8. Are *that/these/this* shoes from Italy?

## Object pronouns

**3** Complete the sentences with *me, you, him, her, it, us,* or *them.*

1. He's my best friend. I really like _him_ .
2. You're my brother but I don't like _____.
3. They're great. We like _____.
4. It's an ugly city. I don't like _____.

5. I'm very happy. She loves _____.
6. She's my manager. I don't like _____.
7. We like them, and they like _____.

## Simple present

**4** Complete the sentences with the verbs in parentheses. Use the simple present.

1. Gary is a chef. He _cooks_ (cook) Italian food in a restaurant.
2. My parents _don't get up_ (not get up) late.
3. I _____ (like) British pop music.
4. We're fashion designers. We _____ (design) shoes.
5. Sophie _____ (not eat) meat.
6. Miguel _____ (eat) a lot of salad.
7. Alex _____ (not like) soccer.
8. You _____ (finish) work late.
9. We are reporters. We _____ (write) newspaper articles.
10. Brian and Tara _____ (watch) TV in the evening.
11. Harry's sister _____ (love) your house.
12. Du-Ho _____ (start) work at ten o'clock.

**5** Write questions and answers with the cues.

1. (Hyun Ok/eat a lot) (yes)
   A: _Does Hyun Ok eat a lot?_ ? B: _Yes, she does._ .
2. (your sisters/like your wife) (no)
   A: _____? B: _____.
3. (you/play tennis) (yes)
   A: _____? B: _____.
4. (they/sell houses) (yes)
   A: _____? B: _____.
5. (Javier/love her) (no)
   A: _____? B: _____.
6. (your friends/live in Barcelona) (yes)
   A: _____? B: _____.
7. (Craig/eat fast food) (no)
   A: _____? B: _____.
8. (we/have any food in the house) (no)
   A: _____? B: _____.
9. (you/design clothes) (yes)
   A: _____? B: _____.

# Time

**6** Write the times in words.

1. _three-forty-five_

2. _____

3. _____

4. _____

5. _____

6. _____

7. _____

8. _____

## can/can't: ability

**7** Put the words in order to make statements and questions.

1. daughter/Can/drive/your
   _Can your daughter drive_ ?

2. can't/Steven/piano/the/play
   _____ .

3. Spanish/speak/They/can
   _____ .

4. you/a/use/Can/computer
   _____ ?

5. dance/can/sing/and/Michelle
   _____ .

6. cook/husband/My/can't
   _____ .

## can: requests

**8** Complete the questions.

1. A: _How_ _much_ _are_ (**1.**) the chicken salad sandwiches?
   B: They're $3.59.
   A: _____ _____ _____ (**2.**) an orange juice?
   B: It's $1.29.
   A: _____ _____ _____ _____ (**3.**) chicken salad sandwich and an orange juice, please?
   B: Certainly. Anything else?
   A: Yes. _____ _____ _____ _____ (**4.**) coffee, please?

2. C: _____ _____ _____ (**5.**) the cheese sandwiches?
   D: They're $3.29.
   C: _____ _____ _____ (**6.**) a piece of chocolate cake?
   D: It's $1.89.
   C: _____ _____ _____ _____ (**7.**) piece of chocolate cake, please?
   D: Certainly. Anything else?
   C: No, thank you.

# Vocabulary

**9** Use the cues to complete the sentences.

1. Do you like _Chinese_ food? (China)
2. Renault is a(n) _____ car company. (France)
3. Giorgio Armani is a(n) _____ fashion designer. (Italy)
4. There are a lot of _____ restaurants in the US. (Mexico)
5. Can you speak _____? (Japan)
6. Younha is a famous _____ singer. (Korea)

**10** Match the verbs to the words or phrases.

_f_ **1.** use      a. an article
____ **2.** write      b. to bed
____ **3.** play      c. TV
____ **4.** design      d. dinner
____ **5.** finish      e. the piano
____ **6.** cook      f. a computer
____ **7.** go      g. work
____ **8.** watch      h. a building

## Vocabulary

**1** Look at the pictures. Complete the crossword puzzle.

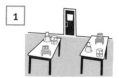 1

 2

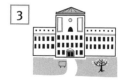 3

 4

 5

 6

 7

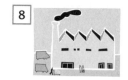 8

**2** Look at the pictures in Exercise 1 again. Write the places. Then write the jobs.

1. _lab_ = _researcher_
2. _____ = _____
3. _____ = _____
4. _____ = _____
5. _____ = _____
6. _____ = _____
7. _____ = _____
8. _____ = _____

## Grammar

**3a** Look at the pictures and use the cues to write imperatives.

1. (quiet)
   _be quiet_

2. (down)
   _____

3. (hold)
   _____

4. (look)
   _____

5. (come)
   _____

**b** Write negative imperatives with the cues. Use *Please*.

1. (sit down) _Please don't sit down_ .
2. (come in) _____ .
3. (turn on your cell phone) _____
   _____ .
4. (look at the next page) _____
   _____ .
5. (watch TV) _____ .

# Communication

**4** Complete the phone calls with the phrases from the box.

> | call back later | I'm sorry | It's |
> |---|---|---|
> | Good afternoon | Certainly | Hello |
> | Hold on, please | How can I | Bye |
> | Can I speak to | | |
> | take a message | | |

### Conversation 1

Receptionist: Good morning. City Hospital.

Woman: Good morning. _Can I speak to_ (1.) Andrew Holden, please?

Receptionist: Certainly. _____ (2.). . .

Receptionist: Hello.

Woman: Hello.

Receptionist: _____ (3.), but Mr. Holden is busy at the moment. Can I _____ (4.)?

Woman: No, thank you. I can _____ (5.).

Receptionist: OK. Thank you. Bye.

Woman: _____ (6.).

### Conversation 2

Receptionist: _____ (7.) North Stone University.

Ted: Good afternoon. This is Ted Miller. Can I speak to Karen Long, please?

Receptionist: _____ (8.) Hold on, please.

Karen: _____ (9.), Karen Long speaking.

Ted: Hello, Karen. _____ (10.) Ted.

Karen: Hello, Ted. How are you?

Ted: Fine, thanks. And you?

Karen: Not bad. Busy as always. _____ (11.) help you?

# Vocabulary

**5a** Complete the months. Then put them in order.

J _u_ l y                    ( 7 )
__ c t __ b __ r             (  )
J __ n __ __ __ r y          (  )
D __ c __ m b __ r           (  )
__ __ g __ s t               (  )
M __ y                       (  )
__ p r __ l                  (  )
F __ b r __ __ __ r __       (  )
N __ v __ m b __ r           (  )
J __ n __                    (  )
S __ p t __ m b __ r         (  )
M __ r c h                   (  )

**b** Cover the months in Exercise 5a. Write the birthday months of the celebrities.

1. Maria Sharapova (04/19/1987) _____April_____
2. Giorgio Armani (07/11/1934) _____
3. Roger Federer (08/08/1981) _____
4. John Travolta (02/18/1954) _____
5. Bruce Springsteen (09/23/1949) _____
6. Bono (5/10/1960) _____
7. Angelina Jolie (06/04/1975) _____
8. Sting (10/02/1951) _____
9. Brooklyn Beckham (03/04/1999) _____

# Vocabulary

**1a** Circle the correct verb.

1. *work*/(*call*)/*write* customers
2. *answer*/*have*/*write* the phone
3. *work*/*travel*/*write* reports
4. *work*/*give*/*have* outdoors
5. *call*/*give*/*answer* presentations
6. *answer*/*travel*/*have* for work
7. *attend*/*write*/*work* meetings

**b** Write the verb phrases below the pictures.

*travel for work*

_____

_____

_____

_____

_____

_____

# Grammar

**2a** Write the words from the box in the correct place.

> ~~often~~   never   usually   sometimes
> not often/not usually   always

100%  a. _____
      b. _____
      c. *often*
      d. _____
      e. _____
0%    f. _____

**b** Put the words in the correct order to make sentences.

1. afternoon/watch/TV/never/I/in the
   _I never watch TV in the afternoon_.
2. work/Maggie/usually/home/doesn't/take
   _____.
3. We/outdoors/work/sometimes
   _____.
4. to/always/go/Do/bed/you/at eleven o'clock?
   _____?
5. golf/He/Sundays/often/plays/on
   _____.
6. for work/They/travel/don't often/
   _____.

**3** Rewrite the sentences with adverbs of frequency.

1. I swim in the ocean.
   (not often) _I don't often swim in the ocean_.
2. I'm late for work.
   (sometimes) _____.
3. I drive.
   (never) _____.
4. I sing and play the piano at family parties.
   (usually) _____.
5. My manager answers the phone at work.
   (not usually) _____.
6. He is happy on Friday afternoons.
   (always) _____.

46

# Reading

**4a** Read the three descriptions. Write the jobs. Then match the jobs to the people.

**1.** _____ Job: _____

Regina doesn't work in an office. She talks to customers a lot but she doesn't usually call them. She always works on Saturdays. She doesn't give presentations or write reports, and she doesn't use a computer.

Regina: "I like my job. I always start work at nine and finish at five. I don't think about my job after five o'clock."

**2.** _____ Job: _____

Darcy doesn't work in an office, and she doesn't work in a school. She sometimes starts work in the morning, sometimes in the afternoon, and sometimes at night. She often works on weekends. In Darcy's job there aren't any customers, but she talks to people every day.

Darcy: "I love my job. I like the doctors, but I don't like the nights."

**3.** _____ Job: _____

Olivia doesn't work in a factory or a lab. She starts work at nine and finishes at five every day. She never works on weekends. She doesn't call customers, but she often sends emails to her students.

Olivia: "My job is OK. I don't love it and I don't hate it."

**b** Read the descriptions again. Complete the sentences with the names of the people.

1. _Olivia_ never works on Saturday.
2. _____ works at a university.
3. _____ doesn't start work at nine o'clock every day.
4. _____ and _____ never call customers.
5. _____ works in a store.
6. _____ works in a hospital.
7. _____ uses a computer at work.

# Writing

**5** Write a note with the phrases from the box.

> Can you    call me at home    Laura
> Hi Jared,    this afternoon?    Thanks,
> My phone number    is 506-555-1312.

Hi Jared,

# Vocabulary

**1a** Complete the crossword puzzle.

## Clues

| Across | Down |
|--------|------|
| **2.** 4th | **1.** 5th |
| **5.** 30th | **3.** 12th |
| **7.** 11th | **4.** 15th |
| **10.** 19th | **6.** 20th |
| **11.** 8th | **8.** 1st |
| **12.** 3rd | **9.** 2nd |

**b** Write the dates using numbers.

1. January twenty-first     *January 21, 1/21*
2. March eleventh     _____
3. May first     _____
4. December twelfth     _____
5. June twentieth     _____
6. November sixteenth     _____
7. September second     _____
8. February third     _____

# Grammar

**2a** Complete the conversation with the phrases from the box.

> I'd like some     What would you like
> thank you     ~~What would you like to~~
> I'd like     Would you like

A: Hello, Mr. Wallace. My name's Orla Birch.

B: Hello, Ms. Birch. This is Mrs. Trenter.

A: Nice to meet you, Mrs. Trenter.

C: Nice to meet you, too.

A: Please, come into my office.
   *What would you like to* (1.) drink?

B: _____ (2.) coffee, please.

C: And I'd like a cup of tea, please.

A: _____ (3.) milk and sugar?

B: No, _____ (4.).

C: Yes, please.

A: _____ (5.) something to eat? A piece of cake?

B: I'd like some fruit, please.

C: _____ (6.) a piece of cake. Thank you.

**b** Write questions and answers with the words in **bold**.

1. A: *Would you like a coffee* ? **coffee**
   B: *No, thank you* . **No**
2. A: *What would you like to eat* ? **to eat**
   B: *I'd like a sandwich, please* . **sandwich**
3. A: _____ . **bottled water**
   B: _____ . **No**
4. A: _____ ? **orange juice**
   B: _____ . **Yes**
5. A: _____ ? **to drink**
   B: _____ . **a cup of tea**
6. A: _____ ? **piece of cake**
   B: _____ . **Yes**
7. A: _____ ? **to eat**
   B: _____ . **a salad**
8. A: _____ ? **iced tea**
   B: _____ . **No**

# Vocabulary

**3a** Put the letters in order to make food words.

1. s g e e t l v a b e      _vegetables_

2. o p s u      s_____

3. d l a a s      s_____

4. k i n d r s      d_____

5. t r u i f      f_____

6. s s e e r t s d      d_____

7. s s k c n a      s_____

8. z p r s t r a e p i e      a_____

9. a c m i s u r o n e      m_____
                        c_____

**b** Complete the story with words from Exercise 3a.

When I go to a restaurant, I always have an

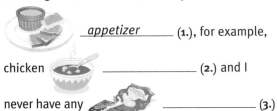 _appetizer_ (**1.**), for example,

chicken _____ (**2.**) and I

never have any _____ (**3.**)

before the meal.

For a _____ (**4.**) I usually

order an Italian dish, for example spaghetti

bolognese with a _____ (**5.**)

or some fresh _____ (**6.**).

I never have _____ (**7.**),

but sometimes I order a plate of fresh

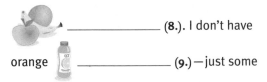 _____ (**8.**). I don't have

orange _____ (**9.**)—just some

bottled water.

# Communication

**4** Read the conversations. Then circle the correct picture for each conversation.

> **Conversation 1**
> A: What would you like?
> B: I'd like vegetable soup, a salad, and chicken, please.
> A: Here you are.
> B: Thanks.
>
> **Conversation 2**
> A: Hello, Mr. Adams. Welcome to our factory.
> B: Thank you.
> A: Would you like a coffee?
> B: Yes, please. With milk and sugar, please.
>
> **Conversation 3**
> A: OK, before the meeting, what would you like to drink?
> B: Can I have a cup of tea, please?
> A: Sure. Would you like a piece of cake?
> B: Yes, please.
> A: Chocolate cake?
> B: Great.

**Conversation 1**

A             B

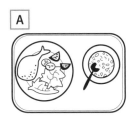 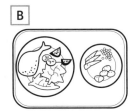

**Conversation 2**

C             D

**Conversation 3**

E             F

LESSON 1

## Vocabulary

**1a** Match the words in the box to the pictures.

| | | | |
|---|---|---|---|
| TV | tennis | reading | swimming |
| eating | biking | soccer | sightseeing |
| ~~chess~~ | theater | hiking | working out |

1. _chess_  2. _____
3. _____  4. _____
5. _____  6. _____
7. _____  8. _____
9. _____  10. _____
11. _____  12. _____

**b** Write verb phrases for the leisure activities in Exercise 1a.

1. _play chess_
2. _____
3. _____
4. _____
5. _____
6. _____
7. _____
8. _____
9. _____
10. _____
11. _____
12. _____

## Communication

**2** Look at the chart. Complete the conversation.

| | Jeff's house | Jorge's house | Mika's house |
|---|---|---|---|
| (TV) | ✓ | ✓ | ✓ |
| (chess) | ✓ | ✗ | ✓ |
| (tennis) | ✗ | ✓ | ✗ |
| (hiking) | ✗ | ✗ | ✓ |
| (working out) | ✗ | ✓ | ✗ |

A: Where do you want to go this weekend?
B: How about Jeff's house. _You_ _can_ _watch_ (1.) TV and _____ _____ _____ (2.) chess at his house.
A: Yeah, but I want to work out. What about Jorge's house? _____ _____ _____ (3.) tennis and _____ _____ (4.).
B: But I want to swim. How about Mika's house. _____ _____ _____ (5.) swimming at her house. She has a swimming pool.
A: Good idea.

## Grammar

**3** Complete the sentences with *want* or *like*.

1. Marcus and Pete _want_ to play soccer.
2. Do you _____ to go out to eat?
3. Which restaurant do you _____ to go to?
4. They don't _____ watching TV.
5. Does she _____ playing tennis?
6. Do you _____ hiking?
7. I don't _____ playing chess.
8. We _____ to go to the theater.

**4** Complete the stories with the verbs in parentheses.

My name is Kate Watson. I'm a chef. I work for a small restaurant called The Happy Chicken. I like _being_ (**1.** be) a chef, and I like _____ (**2.** work) with food. But I don't like _____ (**3.** finish) work at one o'clock in the morning. I want _____ (**4.** work) from nine to five, and I want _____ (**5.** go) out with my friends in the evening. I never see my friends—I'm always at work!

My name is Johan Holland. I'm a construction worker. I like _____ (**6.** build) things, but I don't like my job. It's not exciting. I want _____ (**7.** be) a sales rep. I like _____ (**8.** travel) for work and I like _____ (**9.** sell) things. I don't want _____ (**10.** build) things for eight hours a day.

## Vocabulary

**5a** Rearrange the letters to make adjectives.

1. iiucfdftl = d_ifficult_      4. nuf = f_____

2. yase = e_____      5. netgixic = e_____

3. igrobn = b_____      6. sirtintegne = i_____

**b** Complete the sentences with the adjectives from Exercise 5a.

1. I got 3 out of 20 points on my math test. Math is very _difficult_ for me.

   *Ed Moller, 16, student*

2. I can speak Japanese, English, and Spanish. Languages are very _____ for me.

   *Asenka Chazov, 14, student*

3. I read two or three books every week. Books are very _____ .

   *Armina Lang, 49, lecturer*

4. I don't like having meetings at work. I want to sleep in meetings. They're _____ .

   *Uri Anderson, 42, sales manager*

5. I like traveling and meeting new people. It's _____ .

   *Dan Adams, 26, reporter*

6. I go out with friends from work every Friday evening. It's _____ .

   *Josie West, fashion designer*

## Writing

**6** Read the ad. Then complete the email to the hotel.

# Mountain View Hotel

A beautiful hotel in the heart of the Big Sky country.

- 6 double rooms
- heated swimming pool
- 2 single rooms
- much more!

Come to Mountain View Hotel for a weekend away or a vacation!

mountainviewhotel@montana.net

*bikes, too???*

*breakfast included???*

From: kenchang@worldwidemail.com

To: _mountainviewhotel@montana.net_ (**1.**)

Subject: room for December 18–19

Dear _____ (**2.**)

I _____ (**3.**) some more information about your hotel.

- Do you have a _____ (**4.**) room available for my wife and me on _____ (**5.**)?
- _____ (**6.**) is it for two nights?
- Is breakfast _____ (**7.**)?
- Does the hotel have _____ (**8.**)?

I _____ (**9.**) to your reply.

Yours _____ (**10.**),

Ken Chang

# Vocabulary

**1a** Match furniture words from the box to the pictures.

> sofa   fridge   armchair   dishwasher
> car   stove   cabinet   coffee table
> bed   mirror   bathtub
> sink   toilet

1
sofa

2 _____

4 _____

3 _____

5 _____

7 _____

6 _____

8 _____

10 _____

9 _____

11 _____

13 _____

12 _____

**b** Match the furniture words in Exercise 1a to the rooms.

Bathroom: _____ _____

Bedroom: _____ _____ _____

Kitchen: _____ _____ _____
_____

Living room: _sofa_ _____ _____

Garage: _____

# Grammar

**2a** Look at the chart. Complete Jamie's story.

| | Jamie | Patricia |
|---|---|---|
| bedrooms | 1 | 2 |
| garage | ✗ | ✓ |
| dishwasher | ✓ | ✗ |
| bathtub | ✗ | ✓ |
| sofa | ✓ | ✓ |
| car | ✓ | ✗ |

I _have_ (**1.**) a small apartment in Boston, USA. It _____ (**2.**) one bedroom and a living room. It _____ (**3.**) a garage. I _____ (**4.**) a dishwasher in the kitchen and a sofa in the living room. I _____ (**5.**) a bathtub—just a shower. I _____ (**6.**) a car—it's a small, red sports car.

**b** Look at the chart. Complete Patricia's story.
She _has_ (**1.**) a house in Auckland, New Zealand. It _____ (**2.**) two bedrooms and a garage. She _____ (**3.**) a bathtub in the bathroom and a sofa in the living room. She _____ (**4.**) a dishwasher and she _____ (**5.**) a car.

**3** Complete the conversation.

A: Hello. Can I help you?

B: No, thank you. I'm just looking.

A: Our TVs are on sale today. _Do_ you _have_ (**1.**) a TV?

B: Yes, I _____ (**2.**).

A: _____ you _____ (**3.**) a TV in your bedroom?

B: No, I _____ (**4.**). But I don't want a TV. I want a dishwasher for my mother.

A: _____ your mother _____ (**5.**) a TV in her bedroom?

B: Yes, she _____ (**6.**). Now, how much is this dishwasher?

A: It's $399. The TV is only $299 . . .

**4** Use the cues to write sentences with *have, has, do,* and *does.*

1. (you/a car) (✓)
   A: _Do you have a car_ ?
   B: _Yes, I do_ .

2. (Ravi/a new house) (✓)
   _Ravi has a new house_ .

3. (My parents/a dishwasher) (✗)
   _____ .

4. (your house/a garage) (✗)
   A: _____ ?
   B: _____ .

5. (that hotel/a swimming pool) (✓)
   A: _____ ?
   B: _____ .

6. (my hotel room/bathtub) (✗)
   _____ .

7. (we/a new baby) (✓)
   _____ .

8. (you/a beautiful house) (✓)
   _____ .

9. (my sisters/any children) (✗)
   _____ .

10. (we/any milk in the fridge) (✓)
    A: _____ ?
    B: _____ .

11. (you/an extra pencil) (✗)
    A: _____ ?
    B: _____ .

12. (they/a son named Fred) (✓)
    A: _____ ?
    B: _____ .

# Reading

**5** Read about Jason and answer the questions.

# I want to live in . . .

This week we talk to university professor and writer Jason Thomas.

I want to live In Cuzco in Peru. It's not the capital of Peru, but it's Peru's oldest city. It's interesting and exciting. I love it.

Cuzco is in the south of Peru. It's 800 years old! It has a lot of hotels, stores, and restaurants. My favorite place is the ruins (old city and buildings) of Machu Picchu. It's amazing.

My friends live in Cuzco, and they have a nice house near the center of the city. They also have a small house in the mountains for weekends and vacations.

1. Is Cuzco the capital of Peru?
   _No, it isn't_ .

2. How old is it?
   _____ .

3. What is Jason's favorite place?
   _____ .

4. What is Machu Picchu?
   _____ .

5. Where do Jason's friends go for weekends and vacations?
   _____ .

# Communication

**1** Complete the conversation with *What about . . . ?* or *How about . . . ?* and phrases from the box.

> a swim in the lake
> a game of chess
> that new coffee shop on Baker Street
> seeing a movie
> ~~playing tennis~~

**A:** What do you want to do this afternoon?

**B:** _How about playing tennis_ ? (1.)

**A:** No. I don't like tennis.

**B:** _____
_____? (2.)

**A:** No. I don't like swimming.

**B:** _____
_____? (3.)

**A:** No. I don't want to go to a coffee shop.

**B:** _____
_____? (4.)

**A:** No. I can't play chess.

**B:** _____
_____? (5.)

**A:** Good idea. Which movie?

# Grammar

**2** Complete the questions with question words.

1. **A:** _What_ do you teach?
   **B:** I teach English.
2. **A:** _____ is your favorite actor?
   **B:** Jean Claude Van Damme.
3. **A:** _____ far is your school?
   **B:** It's about 2 blocks from here.
4. **A:** _____ is Jackie?
   **B:** She's in the bathroom.
5. **A:** _____ Elvis song is this?
   **B:** It's "You Are Always on my Mind."
6. **A:** _____ is your teacher?
   **B:** Mrs. Malkmus.
7. **A:** _____ table do you like?
   **B:** I like this table. It's nice.

**3** Read the descriptions. Then write a question for each answer.

Kathleen Stock is a university professor from Cork, Ireland. She's 42 years old, and she works for Dublin City University. Her husband is Tom Stock.

1. **Q:** _What is her last name_ ?
   **A:** Stock.
2. **Q:** _____ ?
   **A:** She's a university professor.
3. **Q:** _____ ?
   **A:** Cork, Ireland.
4. **Q:** _____ ?
   **A:** forty-two.
5. **Q:** _____ ?
   **A:** Dublin City University.
6. **Q:** _____ ?
   **A:** He's her husband.

Iznik is a small restaurant in Denver, Colorado. It serves excellent Turkish food. A typical meal costs $15. The owner is a woman named Ceylan Yildirim. She's from Bodrum in Turkey.

7. **Q:** _____ ?
   **A:** Iznik.
8. **Q:** _____ ?
   **A:** Turkish food.
9. **Q:** _____ ?
   **A:** Denver, Colorado.
10. **Q:** _____ ?
    **A:** $15
11. **Q:** _____ ?
    **A:** Ceylan Yildirim
12. **Q:** _____ ?
    **A:** Bodrum in Turkey.

# Communication

**4** Complete the conversations.

**Conversation 1**

**Waiter:** Hello. Gino's restaurant.

**Sam:** Hello. I'd _like_ (1.) to reserve a table for Saturday evening.

**Waiter:** Certainly. _____ (2.) many people?

**Sam:** Two.

**Waiter:** What _____ (3.)?

**Sam:** Nine o'clock, please.

**Waiter:** And what's the name, please?

**Sam:** Sam Allman.

**Waiter:** OK. _____ (4.) you on Saturday.

**Sam:** Thank you. Good-bye.

**Conversation 2**

**Waiter:** Hello. Do you have a _____ (1.)?

**Sam:** Yes, we do. My name's Sam Allman.

**Waiter:** A(n) _____ (2.) for two?

**Sam:** Yes, that's right.

**Waiter:** _____ (3.) with me, please.

**Waiter:** Are you _____ (4.) to order?

**Sam:** Yes. I'd _____ (5.) chicken soup, please, and lamb chops.

**Waiter:** Certainly. And for you ma'am?

**Tara:** Can I _____ (6.) seafood pasta, please? No appetizer, thank you.

**Waiter:** Certainly. What would you like to _____ (7.)?

**Sam:** Can I have an orange juice, please?

**Tara:** And I'd like some bottled water, please.

_(later)_

**Sam:** Excuse me. Can I have the _____ (8.), please?

**Waiter:** Of course.

# Vocabulary

**5** Look at the pictures. Complete the puzzle to find the secret phrase.

| 1 | L | A | M | B | | |
|---|---|---|---|---|---|---|
| 2 | | | | | | |
| 3 | | | | | | |
| | | | N | | | |
| 4 | | | | | | |
| 5 | | | | | | |
| | | | U | | | |
| | | | R | | | |
| 6 | | | | | | |
| 7 | | | | | | |

# UNIT 9
# Your life

## LESSON 1

## Vocabulary

**1** Correct the phrases.

| Write | Say |
|---|---|
| **1.** 1982 | nineteen and eighty-two <br> _nineteen eighty-two_ |
| **2.** 2009 | two hundred and nine <br> _____ |
| **3.** 1803 | eighteen zero three <br> _____ |
| **4.** 1909 | nineteen hundred and nine <br> _____ |
| **5.** 1970 | nineteen seventeen <br> _____ |

**2** Read the "Fun Facts" article. Then write the details next to the pictures.

> **Fun Facts!**
> - The first TV ad was on July 1, 1941. It was ten seconds long, and it cost just nine dollars.
> - The first newspaper crossword was on December 21, 1913. It was called a "Word-cross."
> - The first cell phone call was on April 3, 1973. It was in New York.
> - The first tourist in space was on April 28, 2001. His name was Dennis Tito.

**1.** _July 1, 1941_
_ten seconds_
_long, $9_

**2.** _____

**3.** _____

**4.** _____

## Grammar

**3** Complete the articles with *was* or *were*.

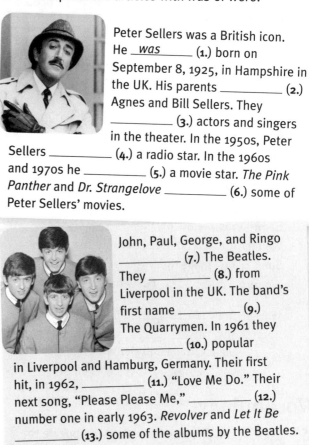

Peter Sellers was a British icon. He _was_ (**1.**) born on September 8, 1925, in Hampshire in the UK. His parents _____ (**2.**) Agnes and Bill Sellers. They _____ (**3.**) actors and singers in the theater. In the 1950s, Peter Sellers _____ (**4.**) a radio star. In the 1960s and 1970s he _____ (**5.**) a movie star. *The Pink Panther* and *Dr. Strangelove* _____ (**6.**) some of Peter Sellers' movies.

John, Paul, George, and Ringo _____ (**7.**) The Beatles. They _____ (**8.**) from Liverpool in the UK. The band's first name _____ (**9.**) The Quarrymen. In 1961 they _____ (**10.**) popular in Liverpool and Hamburg, Germany. Their first hit, in 1962, _____ (**11.**) "Love Me Do." Their next song, "Please Please Me," _____ (**12.**) number one in early 1963. *Revolver* and *Let It Be* _____ (**13.**) some of the albums by the Beatles.

**4** Rewrite the sentences with *was* or *were*.

**1.** Jeff and I are late for the party.
_Jeff and I were late for the party_.

**2.** My son and daughter are at home.
_____.

**3.** I'm a computer engineer.
_____.

**4.** You're my best friend.
_____.

**5.** We're in the garage.
_____.

**6.** Franz is my sister's best friend.
_____.

**7.** This book is really exciting.
_____.

**8.** She's a university professor in London.
_____.

# Communication

**5**  Put the words in the correct order to make sentences.

1. good/When/young,/I was/actor./I was a
   *When I was young, I was a good actor.*

2. she was a/When/beautiful./she was/child,
   _____

3. children,/friends./When they/they were/were
   _____

4. was young,/When he/Tim/very thin./was
   _____

5. you/were you/a child,/When/were/happy?
   _____

6. I was/wasn't/young,/good at/When/I/sports.
   _____

# Vocabulary

**6**  Use the cues and the words from the box to write sentences.

| in | at | of | ~~on~~ | for | with |

1. (Einstein/born/March 14, 1879)
   *Einstein was born on March 14, 1879* .

2. (Alfred Hitchcock/famous/his movies)
   _____ .

3. (Margaret Thatcher/friends/Ronald Reagan)
   _____ .

4. (Martin Luther King Jr. and Spike Lee/born/ Atlanta in Georgia)
   _____ .

5. (Lyndon Johnson/president/the US/ from 1963 to 1969)
   _____ .

6. (Lola Beltrán/good/singing)
   _____ .

# Reading

**7**  Read the webpage. Then mark the statements true (*T*) or false (*F*).

_____ 1. Franklin D. Roosevelt was the first American to win the Nobel Peace Prize.

_____ 2. The first American to win the Nobel Prize for peace was Theodore Roosevelt.

_____ 3. John D. Rockefeller was a billionaire in the UK.

_____ 4. The first World Cup was in Argentina.

_____ 5. The first World Cup winner was Uruguay.

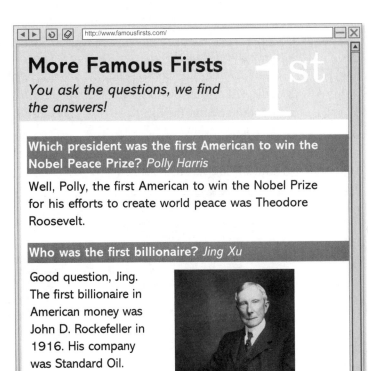

http://www.famousfirsts.com/

## More Famous Firsts   1st
*You ask the questions, we find the answers!*

**Which president was the first American to win the Nobel Peace Prize?** *Polly Harris*

Well, Polly, the first American to win the Nobel Prize for his efforts to create world peace was Theodore Roosevelt.

**Who was the first billionaire?** *Jing Xu*

Good question, Jing. The first billionaire in American money was John D. Rockefeller in 1916. His company was Standard Oil.

**When was the first World Cup?** *Marta Diaz*

The first World Cup was in 1930 in Uruguay. There were 13 countries in the competition. Argentina and Uruguay were the two teams in the final. Uruguay was the winner, 4–2.

# Grammar

**1a** Read the profile. Then use the cues to write sentences.

Cate Blanchett

**PROFILE**

**Name:** Catherine Elise Blanchett
**Born:** May 14, 1969, in Melbourne, Australia
**Father:** Robert Blanchett, from the US
**Mother:** June Blanchett, from Australia
**Childhood:** good actor in high school
**University:** Melbourne University (economics)
**First big film:** *Oscar and Lucinda*
**Children:** Dashiell (born 2001), Roman (born 2004), Ignatius (born 2008)

1. (Cate/born/the US)
   *Cate wasn't born in the US* .
   *She was born in Australia* .

2. (Her father/from/the UK)
   _____ .
   _____ .

3. (She/a good singer/at school)
   _____ .
   _____ .

4. (Her major in school/English)
   _____ .
   _____ .

5. (Her first big movie/*Elizabeth I*)
   _____ .
   _____ .

6. (Her children/born/2002, 2003, 2005)
   _____ .
   _____ .

**b** Write questions with the cues in Exercise 1a. Then write the answers.

1. *Was Cate born in the US* ?
   *No she wasn't* .

2. _____ ?
   _____ .

3. _____ ?
   _____ .

4. _____ ?
   _____ .

5. _____ ?
   _____ .

6. _____ ?
   _____ .

**2** Complete the conversation with *was, wasn't, were,* or *weren't*.

**Interviewer:** So, Melissa, when you _____were_____ (**1.**) a child, _____ (**2.**) you a good singer?

**Melissa:** No, I _____ (**3.**).
I _____ (**4.**) a very bad singer.

**Interviewer:** Who _____ (**5.**) your singing teacher?

**Melissa:** Her name _____ (**6.**) Mrs. Parsons. She _____ (**7.**) great— really great!

**Interviewer:** Who _____ (**8.**) your favorite singers?

**Melissa:** Aretha Franklin and Billie Holiday _____ (**9.**) my favorite singers.

**Interviewer:** _____ (**10.**) your parents singers?

**Melissa:** No, they _____ (**11.**). My mother _____ (**12.**) a scientist, and my father _____ (**13.**) a sales rep.

**3** Correct the mistakes.

1. Was you a good singer when you were young?
   *Were you a good singer when you were young* ?

2. Richard and Alex isn't at work yesterday.
   _____ .

3. I not a math teacher. I was a science teacher.
   _____ .

4. Were Ronald Reagan a movie star?
   _____ .

5. My father not a composer, but he was a musician.
   _____ .

6. Was you at home last night?
   _____ .

7. When were your last vacation?
   _____ .

8. Who your best friend was at school?
   _____ .

9. What were Marlon Brando's last movie?
   _____ .

# Vocabulary

**4a** Read the blog post. Then put the pictures in time order.

> My name is Keiko Tagawa. I work for Trans-Global Software. I travel for work a lot. For example, last week I was in Moscow. Three days ago I was in Athens. Fifteen days ago I was in New York. Yesterday I was in London. Last month I was in Paris.

**b** Complete the phrases with *yesterday*, *ago*, or *last*.

*Today is Wednesday March 24, 2011*

1. March 23, evening = <u>yesterday</u> <u>evening</u>
2. March 17 = _____ _____ _____
3. 2007 = _____ _____ _____
4. March 23, night = _____ night
5. Monday March 15 – Sunday March 21 = _____ _____
6. March 14 = ten _____ _____
7. February 2011 = _____ _____
8. March 23 morning = _____ _____

# Communication

**5a** Complete the conversation with the words from the box. Some words are used twice.

> Would   ~~right~~   was
> wasn't   that

A: Hello. Are you Mr. Sarandon?
B: Yes, that's _right_ (**1.**).
A: I'm Marianne. Nice to meet you.
B: Hello, Marianne. Nice to meet you, too. Please, sit down. _____ (**2.**) you like some coffee?
A: No, thank you.
B: So, you want a job in The Coffee Palace.
A: Yes, that's right.
B: What _____ (**3.**) your last job?
A: I was a sales clerk in a department store.
B: Was that here in Chicago?
A: No, it _____ (**4.**). It was in San Diego. I'm from California.
B: I see. What was the name of the store?
A: Favorite Fashions.
B: Was _____ (**5.**) your first job after high school?
A: No, it wasn't. My first job was in a research lab. That _____ (**6.**) very interesting. It was boring.
B: OK. Can you make good coffee?
A: I can make great coffee . . .

**b** Read the conversation again. Then answer the questions.

1. What does Marianne want?
   _____.
2. Where is The Coffee Palace?
   _____.
3. What was Marianne's last job?
   _____.
4. What is Favorite Fashions?
   _____.
5. Where was Marianne's first job after high school?
   _____.
6. Can she make good coffee?
   _____.

# Vocabulary

**1a** Choose the correct word.

1. (cook)/iron/wash dinner
2. wash/clean/do the laundry
3. iron/vacuum/cook the house
4. cook/wash/clean the bathroom
5. iron/cook/vacuum a shirt
6. cook/iron/wash the dishes

**b** Write housework words from Exercise 1a below the pictures.

A

B

_iron a shirt_ _____

_____

C

D

_____

_____

E

F

_____

_____

# Communication

**2** Complete the conversations with questions from the box.

> How was your flight?    How was school?
> How was your weekend?    How was the party?
> How was your vacation?

1. A: _How was your flight?_ _____

   B: It was OK, but the flight attendants weren't very nice.

2. A: _____

   B: It was good. My teacher likes me!

3. A: _____

   B: It was great. There were 50 people there.

4. A: _____

   B: Fine, thanks. I was in town on Saturday, and I was at home on Sunday.

5. A: _____

   B: It was great. The weather was beautiful, and the food was very nice.

# Grammar

**3** Match the conversations to the pictures.

1. A: Could you carry my suitcase?
   B: Of course.
2. A: Can I use your phone?
   B: Yes, you can.
3. A: Could I have a cup of tea?
   B: Yes, of course.
4. A: Could you take a photo of us?
   B: Yes, sure.
5. A: Could you answer the phone?
   B: Yes, OK.

_____ A

_____ B

_1_ C

_____ D

_____ E

**4** Put the words in the correct order to make requests and ask for permission.

1. you/I/to/Can/talk
   _Can I talk to you_ ?

2. you/dinner/Can/cook
   _____ ?

3. the/Could/open/you/window
   _____ ?

4. down/I/Can/sit
   _____ ?

5. on that report/work/I/tomorrow/Could
   _____ ?

6. on/TV/Could/turn/you/the
   _____ ?

7. help/I/with/you/that/Could
   _____ ?

8. out/I/Can/go/tonight
   _____ ?

**5** Write a suggestion. Use *Could you . . . ?* and phrases from Exercise 1a.

1. A:  _Could you iron my shirts_ ?
   B: Sorry, I can't. The iron is broken.

2. A: _____ ?
   B: Sorry, I can't. The washing machine is broken.

3. A: _____ ?
   B: Sure. What would you like to eat?

4. A: _____ ?
   B: Yes, OK. Where's the vacuum cleaner?

5. A: _____ ?
   B: I can't. The kitchen sink is broken.

6. A: _____ ?
   B: I can't. My brother is taking a shower!

# Writing

**6** Read the letter. Find and correct nine mistakes.

Dear Tesia,

Long time ~~not~~ *no* see. How are you?

Thanks for your last letter. How were your vacation? Our vacation wasn't very good. The hotel was awful, and the weather is very bad.

My family fine, thank you. Viktor is four, and Roza is two year old now. I have a new job. Last year I'm a sales rep, but now I'm a sales manager. The new job is exciting, but I work long hours.

There is a conference in your city next Thursday. I could stay at your house on Wednesday night? I can stay in a hotel, but I want see you.

Could send me an email or call me this week?

Love,

Joanna

## Vocabulary

**1a** Complete the sentences. Then write the verbs in the puzzle to find the secret phrase.

1. You _win_ the lottery.
2. You _____ some money on the street.
3. You _____ a famous person.
4. A police officer _____ you.
5. You _____ to a new house.
6. You _____ your leg.
7. A thief _____ your cell phone.
8. You _____ your wallet or purse.

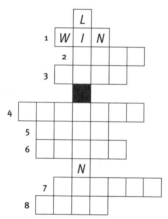

**b** Use phrases from Exercise 1a to label the pictures.

1.

_break your leg_

2.

_____

3.

_____

4.

_____

## Grammar

**2** Complete the email with verbs from the box. Use the simple past.

| | | | | |
|---|---|---|---|---|
| walk | want | cook | ~~start~~ | listen |
| live | play | move | close | talk |

to: lydia.fernandez@fastmail.com
from: irena_miller@epost.co.ca

Hello Lydia,

How are you? The weather here in Madrid is great. Our day _started_ (**1.**) at 7:30 A.M. yesterday! Consuela _____ (**2.**) breakfast for us. Then we _____ (**3.**) to the Prado Gallery. Felipe _____ (**4.**) to see the paintings by Goya and Velazquez. Felipe _____ (**5.**) in Madrid when he was a child, but he _____ (**6.**) to Canada when he was eight years old.

After lunch we _____ (**7.**) tennis in the park. The park _____ (**8.**) at 5:00 P.M. In the evening we _____ (**9.**) to music and _____ (**10.**) about our favorite singers at Consuela's house.

That's all for now. Send me an email and tell me your news!

Love,

Reina

**3a** Complete the article with the correct form of the verbs in parentheses.

# Van Gogh's early life

Vincent Van Gogh _____was_____ (1. be) born in The Hague in Holland in 1853. In 1869 he _____ (2. start) work. Van Gogh _____ (3. work) at an art firm. He _____ (4. not stay) in The Hague. In 1873 he _____ (5. move) to London. He _____ (6. love) a woman named Eugenie Loyer, but she _____ (7. not love) him. Van Gogh was very unhappy. He _____ (8. not like) his job, and in 1874 he moved to Paris. But Van Gogh _____ (9. not stay) in Paris . . .

**b** Use the cues to write questions and answers about Van Gogh.

1. (Van Gogh/move/London)
   A: _Did Van Gogh move to London_ ?
   B: Yes, _he did_ .

2. (Van Gogh/love/Eugenie Loyer)
   A: _____?
   B: Yes, _____.

3. (Eugenie Loyer/love/Van Gogh)
   A: _____?
   B: No, _____.

4. (Van Gogh/like/his job)
   A: _____?
   B: No, _____.

5. (Van Gogh/stay/Paris)
   A: _____?
   B: No, _____.

# Communication

**4** Read the article. Then match the events to the dates.

This is a painting by Paul Gauguin. His full name was Eugene Henri Paul Gauguin. He was born in Paris on June 7, 1848. His family moved to Peru in 1849. In 1855 Gauguin moved back to France with his mother. Many people wonder, Was he friends with Vincent Van Gogh? It's an interesting question. He lived with Van Gogh for three months in 1888. But Gauguin didn't like Van Gogh and he didn't like Van Gogh's paintings. Gauguin moved to Tahiti, in 1895. His wife and children stayed in Europe. Gauguin didn't want to live in Europe, and he loved art from other countries. He worked in Tahiti, but it wasn't easy. He wasn't rich, he was very ill, and the police in Tahiti even arrested him! He died in 1903.

| Events | | Dates | |
|---|---|---|---|
| _e_ | 1. Gauguin was born | a. | 1855 |
| ____ | 2. Gauguin moved to Peru | b. | 1903 |
| ____ | 3. Gauguin moved back to France | c. | 1888 |
| ____ | 4. Gauguin lived with Van Gogh | d. | 1895 |
| ____ | 5. Gauguin moved to Tahiti | e. | 1848 |
| ____ | 6. Gauguin died | f. | 1849 |

# Grammar

**1a** Complete the sentences with the simple past form of the verbs in parentheses.

1. Oliver and Emma ___*bought*___ (buy) a house in Mexico.

2. We _____ (go) to the movies last night.

3. You _____ (see) her. She was at the party.

4. Rachel _____ (say) no.

5. My manager and my wife _____ (meet) your daughter yesterday.

6. He _____ (give) an awful presentation yesterday.

7. Irena and I _____ (find) a beautiful hotel in the center of Kyoto.

**b** Complete the puzzle with the simple past form of the verbs. Some are regular and some are irregular. Find the secret phrase.

1. ~~play~~
2. win
3. lose
4. say
5. come
6. go
7. buy
8. find
9. finish
10. listen
11. meet

| 1 | P | L | A | Y | E | D |

(crossword puzzle with rows 1–11; row 1 = P L A Y E D; shaded column spells down reading ...C...R)

**c** Complete the article with the correct form of the verbs in parentheses.

## Newlyweds win €15 million in Euro Lottery

Janice and Derek Parker from Cornwall ___*won*___ (**1.** win) €15 million in the Euro Lottery last week. Janice and Derek got married on Saturday morning. "We _____ (**2.** not go) on vacation," _____ (**3.** say) Janice. "We _____ (**4.** not have) any money. But we _____ (**5.** go) to a nice restaurant. In the evening I _____ (**6.** look) at the lottery numbers, and I _____ (**7.** be) so happy." And last Friday Derek _____ (**8.** buy) a present for Janice. What _____ (**9.** he/buy) for her? He _____ (**10.** not buy) a new car or a new house. He _____ (**11.** buy) a new dishwasher for her!

**d** Put the words in the correct order to make questions.

1. find/you/your/Did/wallet
   ___*Did you find your wallet*___?

2. Terry/go/out/night/Did/last
   _____?

3. car/they/Did/a/buy/new
   _____?

4. her/Did/love/you
   _____?

5. to/Harry/London/Did/move
   _____?

6. say/"Yes"/Did/you
   _____?

7. lose/passport/you/on/Did/vacation/your
   _____?

8. Did/lottery/win/we/the
   _____?

# Vocabulary

**2** Write the numbers as spoken words.

1. 2,150 – <u>two thousand</u>  <u>one hundred</u>  and
   <u>fifty</u>

2. 1,010 – _____ _____ and
   _____

3. 980 – _____ _____ and
   _____

4. 15,612 – _____ _____
   _____ _____ and
   _____

5. 9,999 – _____ _____
   _____ _____ and
   _____-_____

6. 86,321 – _____-_____
   _____ _____
   _____ and _____-
   _____

7. 115,200 – _____ _____
   and _____ _____
   _____ _____

8. 200,109 – _____ _____
   _____ _____
   _____ and _____

# Communication

**3** Write the words in parentheses as numbers.

**Interesting facts**

1. Mount Everest is <u>8,850</u> (eight thousand eight hundred and fifty) meters tall.
2. About _____ (seven hundred and eighty thousand) people live in Dandong, China.
3. The Nile River is _____ (six thousand six hundred and fifty) kilometers long.
4. Jean Calment died in 1997. She was _____ (one hundred and twenty-two) years old.
5. There are fewer than _____ (ten thousand) red pandas in the world.
6. There are about _____ (six thousand nine hundred) languages in the world.

# Writing

**4** Rewrite the sentences in the correct order.

**News story 1**

A. He married Alexandre Serrano on his 81st birthday.
B. "Rio was very beautiful," he said, "but Alexandre is very, very beautiful."
C. He met her on vacation in Rio de Janeiro.
D. It was a good week for Cristiano Andrade from Portugal.

*It was a good week for Cristiano Andrade from Portugal.*
_____
_____
_____

**News story 2**

A. Now he can't play soccer for six months.
B. They bought soccer player Clive Lightfoot for $2.6 million.
C. Clive arrived at the soccer club on Monday morning.
D. It was a bad week for soccer team Rochdale United.
E. In the afternoon he broke his leg.

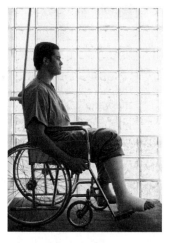

_____
_____
_____
_____
_____

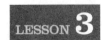

# Grammar

**1** Read the sentences. Then write another sentence. Use the verbs from the box and *be going to.*

> find a new job ~~move~~
> go to the beach go to bed
> break your leg be rich
> cook dinner tonight

1. This country is cold. I *'m going to move* .
2. I went to bed late last night. I _____ early tonight.
3. Estelle doesn't like her job. She _____ .
4. We are on vacation. We _____ this afternoon.
5. You can't ski. You _____ .
6. He's a good businessman. He _____ .
7. She's a great chef. _____ .

**2a** Look at the chart. Complete the sentences about the people.

| Winona and her family: Plans for next year | | |
|---|---|---|
| | **going to** | **not going to** |
| me | eat a lot of vegetables | eat meat |
| my husband | work out | surf the Internet every evening |
| me and my husband | move | stay in our old house |
| my sister | get a new job | go out every night |
| my parents | travel | buy a new car |

1. *I'm going to eat a lot of vegetables* .
   *I'm not going to eat meat* .
2. He _____ .
   He _____ .
3. We _____ .
   We _____ .
4. She _____ .
   She _____ .
5. They _____ .
   They _____ .

**b** Use the cues to write questions for Winona and her family.

1. (you/eat meat)
   Q: *Are you going to eat meat* ?
   A: No, I'm not.
2. (your sister/get a new job)
   Q: *Is your sister going to get a new job* ?
   A: Yes, she is.
3. (your parents/buy a new car)
   Q: _____ ?
   A: No, they're not.
4. (your husband/surf the Internet every evening)
   Q: _____ ?
   A: No, he's not.
5. (Where/you and your husband/move to)
   Q: _____ ?
   A: A big house near his parents.
6. (What job/your sister/get)
   Q: _____ ?
   A: She's going to be a chef.
7. (Where/your parents/travel to)
   Q: _____ ?
   A: They're going to travel to Japan and Korea.
8. (What activity/you and your husband/do)
   Q: _____ ?
   A: We're going to go hiking.

# Communication

**3** Read the answers. Then complete the questions.

1. A: *What are you going to do* next weekend?
   B: I'm not going to do anything next weekend. Why?
2. A: Why _____ learn Spanish?
   B: Because they want to live in Spain.
3. A: _____ a taxi?
   B: No, he isn't. He's going to take the bus.
4. A: _____ wash the dishes tonight?
   B: You are.
5. A: _____ on vacation next month?
   B: No, we aren't. We don't have any money.

## Vocabulary

**4a** Match the verbs with the words to make phrases.

<table>
<tr><td>__d__</td><td>1. learn</td><td>**a.** to college</td></tr>
<tr><td>_____</td><td>2. have</td><td>**b.** a business</td></tr>
<tr><td>_____</td><td>3. start</td><td>**c.** early</td></tr>
<tr><td>_____</td><td>4. get</td><td>**d.** to drive</td></tr>
<tr><td>_____</td><td>5. retire</td><td>**e.** a child</td></tr>
<tr><td>_____</td><td>6. go</td><td>**f.** in shape</td></tr>
</table>

**b** Look at the pictures. What are the people going to do? Use the phrases from Exercise 4a and *be going to.*

1.

_He's going to learn to drive_ .

2.

_____ .

3.

_____ .

4.

_____ .

5.

_____ .

6.

_____ .

## Reading

**5** Read the article and answer the questions.

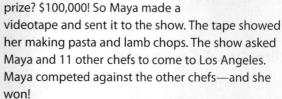

MAYA, a 34-year-old chef from Austin in Texas, loved to cook and wanted to have her own restaurant. But she didn't have any money. So what did she do? She had an idea—to compete on a TV cooking show. The prize? $100,000! So Maya made a videotape and sent it to the show. The tape showed her making pasta and lamb chops. The show asked Maya and 11 other chefs to come to Los Angeles. Maya competed against the other chefs—and she won!

So what is Maya going to do next? She's going to open an Italian restaurant in San Diego. Every day she's going to do what she loves: cook.

Congratulations, Maya!

1. What does Maya love to do?

_____ .

2. What did she want?

_____ .

3. What was her problem?

_____ .

4. What was the answer to her problem?

_____ .

5. What happened?

_____ .

6. Now what are Maya's plans?

_____ .

## Imperatives

**1** Match the words to make imperatives.

_c_ 1. Sit     a. on, please.

_____ 2. Turn     b. off your cell phone.

_____ 3. Listen     c. down, please.

_____ 4. Be     d. at my emails.

_____ 5. Hold     e. quiet, please.

_____ 6. Don't come     f. in.

_____ 7. Don't look     g. to me, please.

## Adverbs of frequency

**2** Rewrite the sentences with the adverbs.

1. I turn off my cell phone.

    (never) _I never turn off my cell phone_ .

2. I'm late.

    (sometimes) _____ .

3. Do you work out?

    (often) _____ ?

4. Are they happy?

    (always) _____ ?

5. I have a coffee in the morning.

    (usually) _____ .

6. She is early.

    (not usually) _____ .

## *like* + gerund/infinitive; *want* + infinitive

**3** Use the cues to write sentences.

1. (Adriana/like/sing)

    _Adriana likes singing/Adriana likes to sing_ .

2. (Peter/want/go out tonight)

    _Does Peter want to go out tonight_ ?

3. (My sister/not like/travel for work)

    _____

4. (Jose and Kay/not want/go swimming)

    _____ .

5. (Alan/not like/play golf)

    _____ .

6. (Sheila and Jeff/like/watch TV)

    _____ ?

7. (I/not want/cook tonight)

    _____ .

## Question words

**4** Circle the correct question word.

1. *What/Where/Who* do you work?

2. *What/Where/Who* do you work for?

3. *What/Where/Who* music do you like?

4. *How/Which/Who* near is it?

5. *How/Which/Where* restaurant do you want to go to?

6. *What/Which/Where* do you do?

## Simple past of *be*

**5** Write questions. Use the past form of *be*.

1. (Where/he born)

    _Where was he born_ ?

2. (What/their names)

    _____ ?

3. (When/you a teacher)

    _____ ?

4. (Where/she yesterday)

    _____ ?

5. (When/your birthday)

    _____ ?

## Permission and requests

**6** Complete the questions with *I* or *you*.

1. Can _you_ spell that, please?

2. Could _____ use your computer?

3. Could _____ open the door for me?

4. Can _____ help you?

5. Could _____ listen to your Billie Holiday CD?

6. Can _____ sing me a song?

## Dates

**7** How do we say the dates below?

1. January 1 _January first_

2. 4/30 _April thirtieth_

3. 12/25 _____

4. March 12 _____

5. 11/13 _____

6. July 4 _____

7. 4/20 _____

8. June 3 _____

## Simple past

**8** Complete the sentences with verbs from the box in the simple past.

> say  ~~arrest~~  get  come  play  lose

1. The police _arrested_ the art thief in the museum.
2. Louise _____ home at twelve o'clock last night.
3. I _____ my wallet last week. There was $30 and my credit cards in it.
4. I talked to my boss about a three week vacation, but he _____ no.
5. I went to bed late last night, and I _____ up late this morning.
6. Danny and Nina _____ tennis yesterday.

**9** Complete the conversations with the simple past form of the verbs in parentheses.

1. A: When _did_ the match _start_? (start)
   B: It _started_ at three.
2. A: What _____ you _____ for lunch? (have)
   B: I _____ a salad.
3. A: Where _____ they _____ to? (move)
   B: They _____ to Australia, but they _____ _____ to Sydney.
4. A: _____ you _____ swimming? (go)
   B: We _____ _____ swimming. We _____ to the park.
5. A: What _____ you _____ in town? (buy)
   B: I _____ some clothes.
6. A: _____ Marlene _____ any photos of you. (take)
   B: No, she _____ But she _____ some pictures of Michael.
7. A: Where _____ Harry and Sally _____? (meet)
   B: They _____ in college.
8. A: Where _____ you _____ her? (see)
   B: I _____ her in a coffee shop on Hudson Street.

## be going to

**10** Use the cues to write complete sentences with *be going to*.

1. (I/not live at home)
   _I'm not going to live at home_ .
2. (Samuel/learn to dance)
   _____ .
3. (We/move to Seoul)
   _____ ?
4. (Mike and Danielle/not come to the wedding)
   _____ .
5. (You/not cook dinner)
   _____ ?

# Vocabulary

**11** Complete the phrases with the verbs from the box. One verb is used twice.

> move    go    break    learn    win
> get    have    start    stay

1. _break_ your leg
2. _____ to college
3. _____ children
4. _____ married
5. _____ a business
6. _____ the lottery
7. _____ to a new country
8. _____ to swim
9. _____ in bed
10. _____ in shape

**12** Match the word to make phrases.

_h_ 1. factory      a. the theater
___ 2. write        b. lab
___ 3. main         c. out
___ 4. go out       d. table
___ 5. work         e. for work
___ 6. go to        f. a meeting
___ 7. coffee       g. to eat
___ 8. travel       ~~h. worker~~
___ 9. research     i. reports
___ 10. have        j. course

# English in Common 1
# Extra Listening Audioscript

The Extra Listening Audio MP3 files and printable Activity Worksheets are provided in both the Student Book *ActiveBook* disc and in the Teacher's Resource Book *ActiveTeach* disc. The link for each unit is found at the top of the Unit Wrap Up page. The audio files are also available at the end of the Audio Program CDs. The audioscripts are also available as printable files on *ActiveBook* or *ActiveTeach*.

# UNIT 1

▶ 2.49

1. **A:** Good afternoon, Mr. González. Welcome to the Eastman Hotel. You're in Room one sixty-three.
   **B:** Room one fifty-three?
   **A:** No, Room one sixty-three.
   **B:** Oh. OK. Thank you.

2. **A:** Hi Cindy.
   **B:** Hi Andy. This is Mara.
   **A:** Hi, Lara. Nice to meet you.
   **C:** Hi. Um. . . . My name is Mara M-A-R-A. Nice to meet you, too.

3. **A:** Where are you from, Mara?
   **B:** I'm from Spain.
   **A:** Really? Where are you from in Spain?
   **B:** I'm from Córdoba.
   **A:** Pardon?
   **B:** Córdoba.

4. **A:** Final call for flight S-R 754 to Tokyo . . .
   **B:** Flight G-X 938 to Rio de Janeiro . . .

# UNIT 2

 2.50

A: This is a great photo!

B: Oh, thanks. It's my family and some friends. She's my mother, Rosa. She's great.

A: She's pretty. What's her occupation?

B: She's a sales clerk in a store.

A: She's young . . .

B: Yeah, she's only 35 years old. And that's my father. He's a police officer. His name is Jaime

A: Jaime?

B: Jaime. J-A-I-M-E. Jaime. He's 41. He's great. And that's my sister, Liliana. She's awful!

A: No, really?

B: Yeah. Really awful. Well, she is 14. That's my brother, Ramón. He's an actor and he's really good. He's an accountant, too.

A: Ooooh. What's his name?

B: That's my best friend, Tomás

A: Wow! He's cute.

B: Yeah. He's a doctor.

A: A doctor? What's his email address . . . ?

B: Uh, María? This is his wife, Constance. She's a teacher.

A: His wife? Oh. Oh, well.

# UNIT 3

▶ 2.51

1. **A:** This thing is in my backpack.
   **B:** Is it big?
   **A:** No, it isn't. It's small.
   **B:** Is it old?
   **A:** No, it's new. It's really modern and beautiful and exciting and. . . .
   **B:** Is it your new MP3 player?
   **A:** Yes!

2. **A:** These things are in my suitcase.
   **B:** Are they sweaters?
   **A:** No, they aren't. They're one thing or two.
   **B:** A pair of shoes!
   **A:** Yes!

3. **A:** It's a museum. It's in New York.
   **B:** Is it a big museum?
   **A:** Yes, it's big.
   **B:** Is it very old?
   **A:** No, it's not old. It's modern. It's very open.
   **B:** Is it The Museum of Modern Art in New York?
   **A:** No, it isn't.
   **B:** Is it the Guggenheim Museum in New York?
   **A:** Yes, it is!

# UNIT **4**

▶ **2.52**

1. **A:** Hi, can I help you?

   **B:** Yes, can I have a cheese sandwich and a small house salad, please?

   **A:** Certainly. Anything else?

   **B:** A small tea, please.

   **A:** For here or to take out?

   **B:** For here. Thanks.

   **A:** OK. That'll be twelve, sixty-five.

2. **A:** Good morning. How can I help you?

   **B:** I have a green and white blouse, and I need a green skirt.

   **A:** OK. What size?

   **B:** Uh, medium. Those are beautiful skirts. How much are those?

   **A:** They're $295.

   **B:** Each?! Oh, dear. Well, how much is *that* skirt?

   **A:** That skirt is on sale. It's $69.

   **B:** Great!

# UNIT 5

▶ 2.53

**A:** And here is room fourteen sixteen.

**B:** Wow, it's a nice big room.

**A:** And there's a beautiful view of Mount Rainier.

**B/C:** Beautiful!

**A:** The bathroom is here and the hot tub is behind the hotel. There's the TV and the TV control.

**C:** Great, thanks.

**A:** Do you have any questions? Seattle is a great place for vacation. There are so many things to do.

**C:** Well, um, are there any good restaurants near here?

**A:** Yeah, there's a great Korean restaurant called Kung-Suh. It's across from the hotel. There are also some good Indian restaurants near here.

**C:** Great.

**A:** And there are great outdoor activities. There's a golf course to the north in Bellevue.

**C:** I can't play golf.

**A:** Ah, too bad. Well there are a lot of good stores in Seattle. There's a famous market—Pike Place Market, by the water. It has great restaurants and great stores. And of course it's Seattle, so there are a lot of coffee shops.

**B:** That's nice. Are there any museums near the hotel?

**A:** Museums? No, there aren't. But there are a lot of art museums in the city. My favorite is the Frye Art Museum downtown. There's free continental breakfast in the morning from six-thirty to eight-thirty. Enjoy your stay.

**B/C:** Thanks!

# UNIT 6

▶ 2.54

A: Nice party.

B: Yeah.

A: My name is Kim.

B: Hi, Kim. My name's Scott. This is my brother, Allen.

A: Hi. You're really brothers?

B: Yes, we're brothers, but we're very different.

C: Yeah, I'm intelligent, handsome, and tall, and Scott's short and ugly. No, just kidding.

A: So, what do you do?

C: I work in a bank and Scott's a chef. Chefs cook food and bankers work with money so I'm rich and he's poor. Well, he's not very rich.

B: Thank you, Allen. I work in an Indian restaurant.

C: The food's pretty bad. I don't like it. Do people really like your food?

B: Yes, they do.

A: Well, I love Indian food! How about music? Do you like the same music?

B: Not really. I like hip-hop music and Allen likes Brazilian music. I like basketball and my brother likes golf.

A: Wow, you are really different!

# UNIT 7

▶ 2.55

1. **A:** Good morning. Can I help you?

   **B:** Good morning. I'm here to see Martha Hernández.

   **A:** Do you have an appointment?

   **B:** Yes, I do. Today is my first day. My name's Tom Murphy.

   **A:** Take the elevator to the fifth floor. Ms. Hernández's office is across from the elevators.

2. **B:** Excuse me. I have an appointment with Ms. Hernández.

   **C:** I'm Martha Hernández. Hello. Are you Tom? Come in. Please, sit down.

   **B:** Thank you. You have a very nice office.

   **C:** Thanks. Would you like some coffee or tea?

   **B:** No, thank you. Uh-oh. Sorry.

   **C:** Please turn off your cell phone. Now. . . .

## UNIT 8

▶ 2.56

A: Please come in.

B: This is a great house.

A: Yes, it is. It's very large and interesting. It has five bedrooms, three bathrooms, a living room, a dining room, a family room, and an exercise room. You can work out here. Do you like to work out?

B: I sometimes work out. Does the exercise room have a bathroom?

A: No. It doesn't. And here we have the kitchen. The kitchen is all new. It has a new dishwasher, a new stove, and fridge. The sink is quite old.

A: It's nice.

B: And look there. You can swim in the pool. Do you like swimming?

A: No, I don't.

B: My husband likes swimming. I don't like swimming. It's boring. I never swim. I like reading and watching TV. I usually watch TV in the evening.

A: Oh. Really?

B: Now the garage. . . .

# UNIT 9

▶ 2.57

A: Hi Yuki! How was your vacation?

B: Hi, Jun. It was great!

A: So, where were you? Were you here?

B: No, I was in California. It was sunny and hot every day. There were beautiful beaches. The water was so blue.

A: Were you with your parents?

B: Yes, I was. And my sister. And my grandmother. She's 87 years old. It was so much fun!

A: How was the food?

B: The food was amazing! And there were a lot of restaurants. My favorite restaurant was a Brazilian place—Ipanema. Fantastic! This was the best vacation. Now, I'm sad it's finished.

A: Oh, well. How was the hotel . . . . . . ?

# UNIT 10

▶ 2.58

**A:** Hi and welcome to "What are you going to do?" On this show, we talk about a difficult problem and ask: "What are you going to do?" OK. Let's begin. Person number one, Imagine this: You find one-hundred dollars on the street. What are you going to do?

**B:** I'm going to ask people on the street near me. I'm going to ask them, "Did you lose this money?"

**A:** You're very honest! Can you tell us why?

**B:** Well, I lost two hundred dollars when I was in college. It was terrible!

**A:** That is terrible. Person number two. You find money. What are you going to do?

**C:** I'm going to buy something with it. Think about it. If I ask someone: Did you lose this money? The answer is going to be Yes.

**A:** OK!? Next problem. Person number three: You win the lottery. You win ten million dollars. What are you going to do?